# First-Year Baby Care

## An Illustrated Step-by-Step Guide for New Parents

**Edited by
Paula Kelly, M.D.**

Meadowbrook Press
Distributed by Simon & Schuster
New York

Library of Congress Cataloging-in-Publication Data
Main entry under title
First-Year Baby Care.
        Includes index.
        1. Infants—Care and hygiene—Handbooks, manuals, etc.
        I. Kelly, Paula, 1949–
RJ61.F47 1983      649'.122          83-8361
ISBN#: 0-88166-255-0
S&S Ordering #: 0-671-56114-6

Published by Meadowbrook Press, Deephaven, MN 55391

BOOK TRADE DISTRIBUTION by Simon and Schuster, a division of Simon & Schuster, Inc., 1230 Avenue of the Americas, New York, NY 10020

Medical Editor: Paula Kelly, M.D.
Managing Editor: Thomas Grady
Writing/Research: Brigitte Frase, Mary Grady, Steve Grooms, Sharon Harrington,
        Mary Francois Rockcastle
Copyeditor: David Tobey
Production Editor: Donna Ahrens
Production Manager: Amy Unger
Writer/Researcher, 1996 Revision: Beth Winters
Text Design: Jay Hanson
Cover Design: Linda Norton
Cover Photo: Elyse Lewin/The Image Bank
Illustrations: Karen Martin and Patricia Carey

The contents of this book have been reviewed and checked for accuracy and appropriateness by medical doctors. However, the authors, editors, reviewers, and publisher disclaim all responsibility arising from any adverse effects or results that occur or might occur as a result of the inappropriate application of any of the information contained in this book. If you have a question or concern about the appropriateness or application of the treatments described in this book, consult your health care professional.

01  00  99            10  9  8  7  6  5

Printed in the United States of America

IN MEMORY OF
**Beth Winters**

## ACKNOWLEDGMENTS

Special thanks to Melissa Avery, C.N.M., M.S.N.; Pamela Barnard; Mavis Brehm, R.N., B.S.N.; Mitch Einzig, M.D.; Kristine Ellis; Robert and Lindsay Collins; Jackson and John Gehan; Michael Grady; Alvin Handelman; Robin, Gregory, and Jasmaine Harris; Gail and Kevin Ketter; Bonnie Kinn; Pat, John, and Kevin Sevlie; Kate and Lily Shank; Sue and Diane Sherek; Peg and Meghan Short; Nancy and Nicholas Wood; and Sue and Sara Veazie.

Thanks also to the Childbirth Education Association of Seattle, for permission to reprint the material on baby exercises. Some of the material in the medical care section first appeared, in slightly different form, in *The Parent's Guide to Baby and Child Medical Care*, edited by Terril H. Hart, M.D. (Meadowbrook, 1982).

# TABLE OF CONTENTS

Introduction . . . . . . . . . . . . . . . . . . . . . . . . . . . . . . . . . . . . . .1

Chapter One: Your Newborn . . . . . . . . . . . . . . . . . . . . . . . .5

Chapter Two: Daily Care for Your Baby  . . . . . . . . . . . . . . .19

Chapter Three: Feeding Your Baby  . . . . . . . . . . . . . . . . . . .49

Chapter Four: Your Baby's Safety . . . . . . . . . . . . . . . . . . . . .77

Chapter Five: Your Baby's Development  . . . . . . . . . . . . . . .91

Chapter Six: Medical Care for Your Baby . . . . . . . . . . . . . .109

Appendix . . . . . . . . . . . . . . . . . . . . . . . . . . . . . . . . . . . . . .159

Index  . . . . . . . . . . . . . . . . . . . . . . . . . . . . . . . . . . . . . . . .166

# Introduction

Becoming a new parent is one of the most thrilling experiences you will ever have. And with it comes a myriad of new responsibilities. *First-Year Baby Care* will help you during the time you'll need it most—your baby's first year. This book's tips and instructions should boost your confidence in your own abilities as a parent or guardian.

New babies grow and change quickly during their first year. Just when you think you've understood one stage, your child will move into another. Every child and every family is unique, of course, but as both a pediatrician and a mother, I've learned that new parents often raise the same questions. They range from simple matters, like how to bathe your baby or child-proof your home, to more complicated ones about daycare, child development, and medical problems.

A team of writers and editors put this book together to answer your questions. They are parents themselves and understand your everyday concerns.

We have published this edition at a time when many new mothers are spending less time in the hospital after their children are born, which gives them fewer opportunities to become familiar with many aspects of new baby care. We hope this text will fill in the gaps. The book is also important to parents who adopt children and may not have access to newborn classes.

We also realize that, as a new parent, you won't have time to read a lengthy text or hunt for information when you need it quickly. We have presented the information you need in an understandable form, and we've supplied illustrations where they are most useful. To make this book accessible to all parents, Chapters 1, 3, and 5 use feminine pronouns; Chapters 2, 4, and 6 use the masculine.

Your baby's first year will challenge you and give you many moments of great joy. I hope this book helps you respond to the trials and appreciate the wonderful new addition to your family.

*Paula Kelly, M.D.*
*St. Paul, Minnesota*

1

# Before Your Baby Arrives

You have to make many decisions before your child is born. A couple of the issues you'll need to discuss are outlined below. Please read about and discuss these questions. And, if you schedule a prenatal visit with the physician or health care provider you've chosen for your baby, you'll have a chance to get acquainted and discuss these matters with him or her. A prenatal visit is also a good time to review any complications you may have had during your pregnancy that might require special attention at birth.

## BREASTFEEDING OR BOTTLEFEEDING

You'll need to decide ahead of time how you plan to feed your baby because your decision will dictate how you'll need to prepare and what you'll need to buy. See Chapter 3 for a full discussion of breastfeeding and bottlefeeding. Should you decide that you are going to breast-feed your child, make sure you read the tips on how to prepare during the last trimester of your pregnancy. (See page 51.)

## CIRCUMCISION

If you have a baby boy, you'll be asked if you want him circumcised, a procedure that normally takes place before he leaves the hospital. You should discuss the pros and cons of circumcision with your health care provider before your baby's delivery and may want to do some more reading on the subject. Controversy continues to surround this issue. In the United States, circumcision is still common, usually for social or religious reasons. Many people are unaware of what the procedure involves and the difference between the appearance of an uncircumcised and circumcised penis. The uncircumcised baby's skin, called the foreskin, completely or nearly completely covers the end of the penis. The circumcision procedure, which should only be performed by an experienced physician, removes some of this tissue. Your baby may receive a local, injected anesthetic to decrease his pain and stress.

The American Academy of Pediatrics (AAP) has stated, "Newborn circumcision has potential medical benefits and advantages as well as disadvantages and risks." Some potential benefits include a possible decreased incidence of cancer of the penis in males and decreased chance for cervical cancer in their female sex partners. The incidence of sexually transmitted diseases may also be decreased in circumcised males, and some studies suggest urinary tract infection may be less likely as well.

A baby who is very premature or ill, or who has an abnormality in the development of the penis, should not undergo a circumcision. Bleeding problems and infection can occur. Consider the procedure more carefully if your family has a history of bleeding problems. Furthermore, some have speculated that circumcision may have a decreased effect on sexual pleasure.

## HOME HEALTH CARE

In these days of shorter hospital stays after childbirth, parents are often concerned that their babies may need more medical attention than they're getting, and new parents often struggle with the feeling that they don't know how to perform the basics, such as breastfeeding. If you have some of these concerns, consider arranging a home visit by a nurse in the days following your return from the hospital. Nurses with surgical or obstetrics backgrounds can help new parents understand how to meet a baby's needs and advise when further medical attention is needed. Some health care plans cover a portion of the expense.

## PRACTICALITIES

In addition to the above decisions, make sure you've got everything you'll need during the first few weeks after your baby is born. You're not likely to have the time or the energy to take shopping trips with a newborn. In various sections of the book, you'll find information to help you make safe, sensible choices. On page 26 you'll find tips to help you decide what type of diapers you'll need, and on pages 42–46 are recommendations on clothing a new baby. On page 84 you'll read about outfitting a crib, and on pages 83–87, you'll learn about what to look for when you buy equipment for your child. Read about car safety on page 83, and make arrangements before your baby is born to have an approved car seat for the trip home from the hospital; be sure his first trip in a car is as safe as it can be.

# CHAPTER 1

# Your Newborn

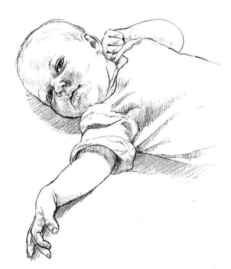

If you're a first-time parent, you've probably been spending lots of time learning about the intricacies of pregnancy and childbirth, practicing your breathing techniques (or coaching your partner), and worrying about how you'll hold up during labor and delivery. You've been concentrating—and rightly so—on the big day, the birth of your child. You've been preparing to breathe a big sigh of relief when it's over and you're able to hold a healthy baby in your arms.

The memories of pregnancy and your child's birth will not fade soon; in fact, you'll probably sharpen those memories by telling any willing listener the whole story of your labor and delivery in glorious detail. The presence of a newborn, however, immediately puts the experience into a brand new perspective. The baby you had gotten used to being "in there" is now "out here." You realize your pregnancy was just the beginning, not an end in itself.

The year you're just beginning with your baby will be full of firsts—the first smile, the first tooth, the first word, the first step.

When you look back over this year, you'll be amazed at how your child has grown and changed, and you should be proud of what you've learned and accomplished. Your baby will need much care and attention as she makes the transition from the world inside the womb to the one outside it. The process of this transition is one with monumental consequences for both the parents and the new baby.

## CHANGES FOR THE PARENTS

For you as a parent, the birth of your child means, for a start, less free time and virtually no time for spontaneity. You'll have fewer opportunities to go out to a movie or dinner, and such evenings will almost never happen at a moment's notice. You'll find that you need to choose sitters in advance and plan around the baby's schedule. And you'll deliberate far in advance about how long you can be away from home. Once you've walked out the door without your baby (and not without a little trepidation), you'll find yourself thinking and talking of nothing but your child.

No one is going to pretend a newborn

doesn't place a great deal of stress on a couple's relationship—especially if the child is your first. You'll find that even if you share the diapering and bathing and rocking and burping, the entire day *seems* taken up by caring for the baby. And there will be times when child care seems to consume your entire night as well, as you walk the floor with an infant who hasn't figured out the difference between day and night.

Babies are notoriously unpredictable. In the middle of a long-awaited meal, or some too-long-postponed lovemaking, or even a much-needed phone conversation with a supportive friend—suddenly your baby needs you, and *now*. But if you're like most parents, "demand" is too harsh a word for this situation. Your baby needs you, so you go, and gladly. Few things in life are more satisfying than a growing confidence in your ability to comfort your child and provide the nurturing she needs.

Both parents come to know dozens of joys and worries during the first weeks of their baby's life, but the mother is especially vulnerable in those postpartum days. The tremendous hormonal changes that a woman experiences can contribute to depression, sometimes making it difficult for her to enjoy her newborn as much as she otherwise would. Eating right, gradually increasing exercise after giving birth, and sleeping when the baby sleeps will work to combat postpartum blues for a new mother. A support system of family, friends, or other new parents will also ease the adjustment.

Furthermore, if the newborn is not the first child, parents will almost inevitably contend with a case or two of sibling rivalry. No matter how well you've prepared your other child for the newborn, he or she may still suffer a slight regression—a normal response to the startling realization that he is no longer an only child. The older child may suddenly want to take a bottle or start nursing again. His nightly sleep pat-

terns may become disturbed. He may take to sucking his thumb or wetting his pants, even if he showed all signs of being successfully toilet trained. Again, this kind of reaction is common, and is simply your older child's way of requesting the love and attention he's afraid the new arrival will deprive him of.

## CHANGES FOR THE BABY

Unquestionably, parents have a great deal of adjusting to do with the birth of their child. But the newborn is forced to make a transition from the ideal environment of the uterus to the harsher and certainly more varied world outside the mother's womb. Whether your baby was born vaginally or by cesarean, she went through an intense, exhausting physical experience. She'll need some time to adjust to her new world. In fact, at birth, in response to the exhaustion of the birth process, most newborns enter into a six-hour sleeping period, from which it's difficult to wake them.

Consider these other facts about newborns:

- A newborn normally weighs between six and eight pounds (2.7 and 3.6 kg) and is eighteen to twenty-two inches (45 to 55 cm) long at birth. Typically, however, she'll lose up to 10 percent of her weight in the days following birth, then start to regain that weight by the end of her first week.

- A baby spends her entire first nine months of existence passively receiving all of her nourishment through the umbilical cord. Until birth, a newborn has never had to swallow to appease her hunger. In fact, she's never known what hunger is.

- Before her birth, a newborn has never had to breathe, because she received all of her oxygen through her mother's blood. At birth, although her heart may beat 120 times a minute, her circulation is still sluggish, and her breathing is shallow and irregular. She'll also sneeze, gasp, hiccough, and cough. You may think these are cold symptoms, but it's just the newborn's way of clearing mucus from the respiratory system.

- Having been perfectly insulated inside her mother's body, a newborn has never known cold or heat. Her skin has been constantly bathed in amniotic fluid, so she has never felt a rush of air or a sharp poke. At birth, however, her temperature drops rapidly in response to the outside air, and others must ensure that she stays warm.

- While a newborn was in the womb, all outside sound was muffled for her by layers of fluid, blood, and tissue, so she's been ignorant of sharp, loud noises. Her sleeping and waking schedule has been entirely her own, because she has had no need to distinguish day and night. And the most constant, familiar movement she has known, as she has been lodged in the cradle of her mother's body, has been the gentle rocking created by her mother's daily movements.

It's no wonder, then, that a newborn may take a few weeks to adjust. She's just been born into a world in which she suddenly needs to eat, defecate, and breathe, and is expected to sleep on schedule and be cuddled and held. In spite of all that babies go through to survive, and all that parents must do and experience in order to help them survive, the first year of life is a marvelous adventure. Babies *do* thrive, and the love of their parents never ceases to grow.

# Characteristics of a Newborn

You've probably seen enough photographs of newborns to know they are generally not the cute, cuddly creatures they will grow to be after three or four months. What follows are descriptions of characteristics typical to newborns that you can expect to see in the days immediately following birth.

## HEAD

The head of a newborn may look lopsided and may be molded into a pointy melon shape by the pressures of the birth canal. It is large in proportion to the body—about one-fourth of the body length. The neck is short and creased. A tough membrane covers the head's two soft spots, called *fontanels,* where the bones of the skull have not yet fused. The anterior fontanel, the larger one at the top near the front, closes after eighteen to twenty-four months. The posterior fontanel, at the top near the back, closes by six months.

It's impossible to predict how much hair a newborn will have or keep. Some have no hair or a short crop that will fall out and be replaced after about six weeks. Others have lots of locks and may never lose them.

## FACE

A newborn's eyes will probably be red and puffy from the pressures of birth and from drops or ointment that may have been used. Light-skinned babies usually have blue-gray eyes, and dark-skinned babies usually have brown eyes. Permanent color won't develop for about six months. Tears may be present from birth, but don't appear in most babies until six weeks or so.

The nose of a newborn, which consists entirely of cartilage, appears flat and broad. The cheeks are usually fat, and the face will sometimes appear chinless.

## SKIN

The skin of a newborn is wrinkled and loose, and it may start to look dry and start peeling after a few days. A newborn's body may be covered with *vernix caseosa,* a white, waxy substance that has eased the baby's movement through the birth canal. The body may also still have *lanugo,* a downy fuzz over the shoulders, back, and cheeks. This soft hair will disappear within a few days.

The color of the skin usually fluctuates for the first few days, ranging from purple-blue to pink to gray. Newborns of African, Asian, or Mediterranean descent often have light skin that will later turn dark.

## BODY

The abdomen of a newborn is large, with small hips and a body that curls inward. An umbilical stump is present where the umbilical cord has been cut from the navel. The stump will dry up and fall off on its own, most often between ten and fourteen days after birth. (See page 34 for how to care for the newborn's navel.)

The breasts and genitalia of a newborn may be swollen in both sexes due to the presence of hormones from the mother, and baby girls may bleed slightly from the vagina. This swelling most often disappears in three to five days. Urine and stool will usually appear within the first twenty-four hours. (See page 23.)

## ARMS

A newborn's arms are flexed. The hands, which are generally cool and curled into fists, may look blue because of an immature circulatory system. The wrists may be fat and creased, and the fingernails may be long and sharp. (See page 35 for how to trim an infant's fingernails.)

## LEGS

The knees of a newborn are bent and the legs are bowed. Like the hands, a newborn's immature circulatory system may cause the feet to look blue. A newborn's feet are also mottled and may appear flat because of fat pads on the soles.

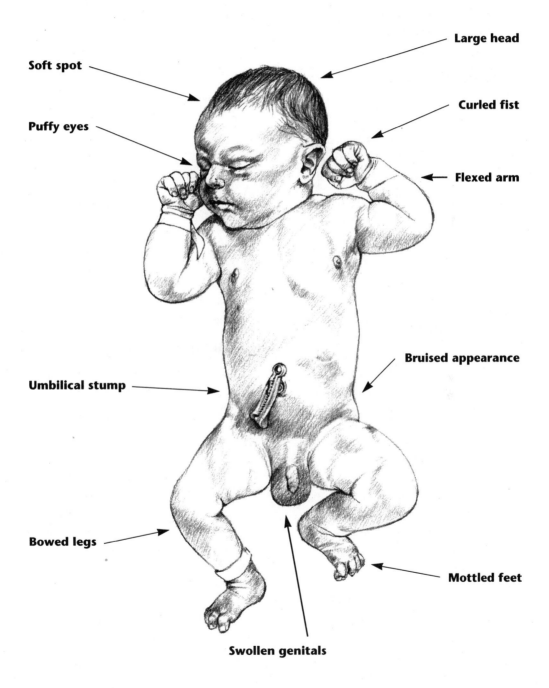

**Large head**

**Soft spot**

**Curled fist**

**Puffy eyes**

**Flexed arm**

**Bruised appearance**

**Umbilical stump**

**Bowed legs**

**Mottled feet**

**Swollen genitals**

# Conditions That May Be Present at Birth

Even after a normal birth, your baby may have one or more medical conditions, most of which are no cause for concern. The following list describes conditions that may be present at birth, and that most often heal or disappear with time.

## BIRTHMARKS

Some birthmarks may be present at birth, while others may develop in the first month of life. They are very common and should be no reason for concern. Most birthmarks disappear or fade on their own by the time your child is school aged.

## LIP BLISTERS

You may notice a blister on your baby's lips, caused by intense sucking. Don't worry; these blisters are normal and are not painful.

## TEARS AND BLOCKED TEAR DUCTS

A membrane covers the tear-making tissue at birth, so real tears may not appear until weeks after birth. In some cases, a condition where the ducts that drain the tears are blocked also occurs, leading to excessive tearing and even infection in one or both eyes. Usually the ducts open spontaneously with time. Sometimes drops are prescribed to help clear out a secondary discharge that can accumulate. If the blocked ducts persist and cause symptoms, surgery may be indicated near the end of the first year.

## BROKEN CLAVICLE (COLLAR BONE)

A vaginal birth sometimes results in a fractured collar bone. Even without special constraints, it will heal over time.

## DISLOCATED HIPS

It is fairly common for newborns to be born with dislocated hips, or to develop them in the days and weeks following birth. Your physician should try to detect this condition as early as possible during your regular visits, and treat it if necessary.

## HEMATOMA

A hematoma is a swelling of fluid beneath the scalp, caused by pressure of the baby's head against the pelvic outlet. Your newborn may have several that look like big "goose eggs," but don't worry. They most often disappear in about a week.

## MILIA

Milia are undeveloped or blocked sweat glands that may show up as white, pinpoint spots on the nose, chin, and cheeks. They disappear over time.

## NEWBORN JAUNDICE

Jaundice refers to the yellow color in a baby's skin. It is a condition that often appears within a few days after birth and disappears within a week. This process is normal and should not ordinarily be a cause for concern. The yellow color is the result of *bilirubin*, a by-product of the breakdown of red blood cells. All of us have "old" red blood cells that break down, but newborns have more of them and their immature livers are somewhat slow in processing the bilirubin.

Only rarely is newborn jaundice a cause for concern. If it is, your physician will monitor the level of bilirubin with blood tests after birth. If it persists beyond five to seven days after birth, further evaluation may be necessary. If the skin becomes jaundiced to a fair degree, it may be necessary to treat the condition by putting the newborn under "bilirubin lights," or under a special blanket-like device used to lower the level of bilirubin. Also, about 5 percent of breast-fed babies have prolonged jaundice, probably because of the fatty acids in breast milk. Only on rare occasions should the mother temporarily stop breastfeeding because of jaundice. If she does, the mother should pump her breasts to maintain a steady milk supply. (See page 53.)

## NEWBORN RASH

Before they are a few days old, rashes affect many babies. Splotches or pimples often appear on the chest, back, or face and disappear without treatment.

## PIGEON TOES

Also known as intoeing, this condition may be common in newborns because of their position in the uterus. Pigeon toes usually correct themselves before the end of the first year. Most physicians do not recommend treatment in the first year unless it is accompanied by other foot deformities.

## TONGUE TIE

The fold of the skin attaching the tongue to the base of the mouth may be longer and thicker than usual, inhibiting the tongue's forward movement. This condition needs no correction and will not lead to eating or speech problems.

## WRIST LESIONS

Fetal sucking produces these lesions. They will disappear without treatment over time.

# Newborn Exams

Your newborn will undergo a variety of procedures in the hospital. Some take place immediately after birth, and some are delayed until right before you're discharged from the hospital, when your infant is more settled. All of these procedures are routine and are no cause for alarm.

## EYE CARE

When a baby passes through the birth canal, the eyes are susceptible to any infections that may be present in the mother. Some of these infections can cause blindness, and because they are easily prevented, a doctor or nurse commonly administers eye drops or ointment in the delivery room at birth.

## APGAR TESTS

Immediately after a hospital birth, a doctor or nurse will evaluate your baby using the Apgar scale (see below), which provides an indication of your baby's well-being. Your health care provider will observe the newborn's heart rate, respiratory effort, muscle tone, reflex irritability (or response), and skin color, and will record a score of zero to two for each of these five areas. Readings are recorded at one minute and again at five minutes after birth. Don't be overly concerned about your baby's performance here: a perfect score of ten is unusual, and scores over seven are perfectly okay. Even lower scores are seldom cause for alarm.

## NEWBORN EXAM

Typically, a physician will examine your baby thoroughly within twenty-four hours of birth. If you are in the hospital more than one day, your baby may get a second examination prior to discharge. If possible, attend one of these exams. They provide an excellent opportunity for you to ask questions and learn. The doctor will check your baby from head to toe, listen to her heartbeat, feel her pulse, test for dislocated

| SIGN | 0 | 1 | 2 |
|---|---|---|---|
| **Heart Rate** | Absent | Slow (below 100 beats per minute) | Over 100 beats per minute |
| **Respiratory Effort** | Absent | Slow, irregular | Good, crying |
| **Muscle Tone** | Limp, flaccid | Some flexing of extremities | Active motion |
| **Reflex Irritability** 1. Response to stop on foot | No response | Weak cry or grimace | Rigorous cry |
| 2. Response to catheter in nostril | No response | Grimace | Cough or sneeze |
| **Color** | Blue, pale | Body pink, extremities blue | Completely pink |

hips, check her reflexes (see pages 16–18), and examine the inner organs that can be felt through her soft skin. The examining physician may also determine more exactly what your baby's gestational age is, concluding whether your baby is preterm or post-term.

## SCREENING TESTS

Through screening tests, a doctor or nurse will check your baby for several diseases that have no visible symptoms, but that could cause serious damage. He or she will draw a few drops of blood from your baby to test for them.

- Phenylketonuria (PKU). Occurring in one infant in 12,000, PKU is a hereditary disease that causes mental retardation. Unaffected parents can pass on PKU, which is caused by the body's inability to digest protein normally. Treatment consists of putting the baby on a special diet that's low in phenylalanine, the part of the protein that the body can't digest.

- Galactosemia. Also carried by unaffected parents, this disease appears in one infant in 50,000. It occurs when the body cannot use milk sugar (lactose) normally. It can cause mental retardation, cataracts in the eyes, and an enlarged liver. Treatment consists of a nondairy diet.

- Hypothyroidism. This condition occurs in one infant in 4,000 and results in growth problems, mental retardation, and lethargy. A defect in the thyroid gland causes hypothyroidism, which is treatable with hormone medication.

- Congenital Adrenal Hyperplasia. The incidence of this disease is about one in 15,000. It is a genetic disorder that results in a hormonal imbalance. It can cause sexual development problems, hormone problems, and death if not treated with replacement hormones.

- Hemoglobinopathy. This disease causes changes in red blood cells. Sickle cell disease is the most common form of hemoglobinopathy, and it can cause anemia (a low red blood cell count) as well as other serious problems. In the African American population, one in 500 babies has sickle cell disease. Other forms of hemoglobinopathy can also be detected. Medical monitoring and intervention are critical for treatment of some forms, while others are asymptomatic.

# Your Newborn's World

Until fairly recently, scientists thought newborns were naturally passive and uninvolved with their surroundings—little "blank slates" waiting for the world to form them. Today, researchers are finding ways to discover what is going on inside the heads of newborns, and they are learning that newborns are remarkably responsive and complete little people. They perceive the world almost as well as adults, and they're keenly interested in it—especially in people. The more newborns are studied, the more extraordinary they prove to be.

Here's a brief description of how a newborn's senses and other faculties function at birth.

## TOUCH

Newborns are exceptionally aware of touch, probably more so than adults. Touch has been called "almost a language" for infants, who readily perceive small changes in texture or temperature. More than any other sense, touch allows a developing baby to relate to its surroundings before birth, which is why it is such an important sense early in life.

Newborns react with pleasure to warm, soft, firm pressure, especially on the front surfaces of their bodies. Holding them closely or swaddling them (see how on pages 20–22) will often calm them. Recent research indicates that close physical contact between mother and child in the first weeks of life is very important to the newborn's sense of well-being. In fact, the bonding that takes place between the mother and her newborn in the first hours of life is not only desirable, but might aid the baby's development in ways that can be measured several years afterward.

Recognizing the importance of parent-infant bonding, many childbearing couples want to spend as much time as they can with their newborn immediately after birth. Hospitals are relaxing the routines that used to interfere with this kind of interaction. Cuddling, kissing, touching, lots of eye-to-eye and skin-to-skin contact, and other physical manifestations of affection are a wonderful way for both parents to begin their relationship with their baby as soon as she arrives. The mother who chooses to breast-feed her baby can establish that special relationship with her child within minutes or hours of birth.

## SIGHT

Although newborns can see from the moment of birth, they are extremely nearsighted. Their eyes are like simple cameras with the focus fixed at about eight to twelve inches (20–30 cm). That is the distance, not coincidentally, between a mother's and a newborn's face when the baby is being cuddled or nursed. Beyond that distance, newborns perceive only brightness and movement. They can track an object moving slowly from side to side, or with more difficulty, an object moving up and down.

By two months, your baby should track objects that move slowly in front of the line of vision. If you have any concerns about your baby's sight, raise them with your health care provider. Babies can be tested even as newborns, if there's any reason to suspect a problem. Crossed eyes, however, are normal during the early part of infancy. (See page 134.)

Babies observe the world with limited vision but unlimited interest. Newborns will drop their mother's nipple in the delivery room to stare at an attractive object. Shortly after birth, babies are most attracted by complex, highly patterned, visual objects. Surprisingly, they are more sensitive to black and white graphics than to color. Within weeks, though, they would rather look at faces than anything else. (To a newborn, an object is a face if it is round and has a hairline, eyes, and a mouth.)

## HEARING

Babies are born with a well-developed sense of hearing. Within ten minutes after birth, they can locate the source of a sound. They seem to respond to sounds lasting ten seconds, but not to sounds lasting only a second or two. Newborns seem so intrigued by sounds even at birth that they will discontinue sucking to pay better attention to an attractive sound. Just moments after birth, newborns will seem to display definite preferences in sounds. They especially like high-pitched voices and sounds that are rhythmic and soft. As parents, you should talk and even read to your baby.

An infant should move or be startled (see page 16) in response to a loud noise. If you have any questions about your child's hearing, raise them with your physician. (See hearing loss, page 143.)

## SMELL AND TASTE

The senses of smell and taste are essentially the same for infants. Less is known about what babies can smell and taste than about their other senses, primarily because researchers find it difficult to tell when a baby is discriminating between one smell or taste and another. Newborns *do* react to sweet, sour, and salty tastes. They are obviously upset by foul odors. And they can differentiate among plain, slightly sweetened, and very sweet water.

## INTELLIGENCE

Babies are born knowing little or nothing. They seem to lack specificity in responses—meaning that they react with an identical response, such as finger sucking, to a wide variety of stimuli. A single change in a newborn's environment, such as a drop in temperature, will often cause its whole body to react. Newborns have such short memories that objects are not remembered unless they reappear within two-and-a-half seconds.

Yet babies are anything but intellectually passive. Their interest in their surroundings is keen and discriminating. They can choose to pay attention to a single object in their environment. Even when they are quite young, babies combine touch, sight, and hearing into meaningful patterns.

## SOCIABILITY

Most remarkably, babies seem programmed to take an interest in the people who surround them, although they are born knowing nothing about the existence of other beings. Newborns crave contact—by touch, sight, smell, and hearing—with people, especially their parents. By one week they might recognize the sound of a parent's voice, and by two weeks they can know their parents, especially their primary caregivers, by sight. Babies only four weeks old sometimes behave differently with their parents than with other people.

# Newborn Reflexes

A newborn's reflexes are her spontaneous, automatic responses to external or internal stimuli. They are the building blocks of intelligence and the foundation of physical coordination. Some reflexes, such as gagging and blinking, remain throughout life. Others, such as grasping and walking, disappear, or "go underground," only to reemerge later as consciously controlled activities. The physician who examines your baby will check for the presence of some of these reflexes as indications of a healthy nervous system.

| REFLEX | WHAT TRIGGERS IT | DESCRIPTION | APPEARANCE/ DISAPPEARANCE |
|---|---|---|---|
| **Startle (Moro)** | External stimuli such as sudden changes in light, noise, movement or position.<br><br>Internal stimuli such as the baby's own crying or muscle twitches during sleep. | An infant will fling out the arms and legs, then quickly pull them into the chest while the body curls, as if to cling. | Tapers off in 1 to 2 weeks and disappears by 6 months. |
| **Sucking** | Touching a part of the baby's mouth or cheek with a nipple or finger. | The baby's lips pucker while her tongue curls inward to pull. | Strongest in the first 4 months. After 6 months it fades, merging gradually with conscious activity. |
| **Rooting** | Stroking a cheek or an area around the mouth. | The baby's head turns in the direction of the stroking and searches with the lips for a nipple. The baby uses this reflex to seek food. | Continues while the baby is nursing. |

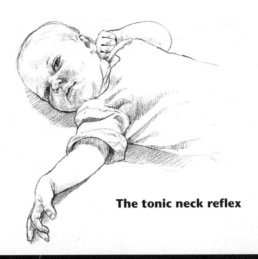

**The tonic neck reflex**

| REFLEX | WHAT TRIGGERS IT | DESCRIPTION | APPEARANCE/ DISAPPEARANCE |
|---|---|---|---|
| **Grasping** | Stroking the hands or pressing the balls of the feet at the base of the toes. | The baby's fingers curl as if to hold onto an object, or the toes curl. | Decreases noticably after 10 days and usually disappears around 4 months. May continue in the feet until 8 months. |
| **Stepping** | Holding the baby in a standing position and pressing down a little. | The baby lifts each foot in turn, as if to walk. | Diminishes after 1 week and will disappear in about 2 months. |
| **Placing** | Holding the baby's shins in contact with an edge. | The baby tries to step upward to put her feet on the surface of a table or bed. | Disappears in about 2 months. |
| **Tonic neck** | Laying the baby on her back. | The baby's head is turned to one side while lying on her back. The arm on the side that the face is turned toward extends straight out, and the other arm flexes in a kind of fencer's pose. | Most obvious at 2 to 3 months and disappears at around 4 months. |

| REFLEX | WHAT TRIGGERS IT | DESCRIPTION | APPEARANCE/ DISAPPEARANCE |
|---|---|---|---|
| **Blinking** | Bright light, touching an eyelid, or sudden noise. | The baby's eyelids open and close rapidly. | Permanent |
| **Gagging** | Foreign matter in the respiratory system. | The baby chokes, gasps, spits up, and may turn blue. (Even when the head is under water, the reflex in most cases prevents infants from breathing in.) | Permanent |
| **Swallowing** | Food in the mouth. | The baby's trachea closes while the esophagus opens. | Permanent |
| **Withdrawal** | Pain, cold air. | The baby tries to pull away while drawing in limbs close to the body. | Permanent |
| **Parachute** | "Diving" your baby toward the floor. | The baby extends hands out for personal protection. | Appears around 7 months after birth. |

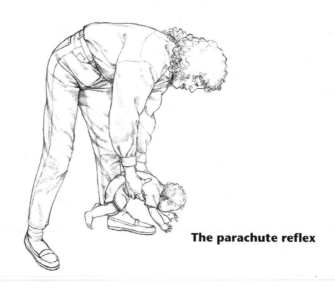

**The parachute reflex**

# CHAPTER 2

# Daily Care
# for Your Baby

As you go about the daily routine of bathing your baby, changing diapers, dressing and undressing him, comforting him when he's fussy, and putting him to sleep, his complete dependence on adult caretakers will be on your mind occasionally. This dependence won't change much during the first year. Left alone, your child will be just as incapable of changing his own diaper at one year of age as he was at one week.

Before you change your first diaper, you're liable to feel just as helpless as your baby. You'll be nervous—especially if you're under the eye of a well-meaning but intrusive neighbor or relative—and each movement will seem awkward and unnatural. Bath-time may also give you the shakes, and dressing your infant for a first outing may seem to require a minimum of four hands.

The purpose of this chapter is to get you through this early stage. With the instructions that follow (which you may only have to refer to once) and inevitable practice, you'll soon be able to change diapers in your sleep. (In fact, you probably will once in a while.) Along with the basic skills, you'll develop a great deal of patience, the dexterity necessary to do more than one thing at a time, and the resourcefulness required to amuse a baby who's undergoing his umpteenth diaper change. This sort of care gives both mother and father the chance to establish a special parent-child relationship. Bathing and diapering allow you to hold and make plenty of eye contact, to sing special songs, and to play silly games. And rocking your baby to sleep can be one of the most blissful activities of your day. Once you can relax at these tasks, you'll come to know the real joys of meeting your baby's basic needs.

The last page of this chapter describes how to find a reliable caretaker for your baby—what to look for in a day-care provider who has the same confidence, competence, and patience you develop.

# Handling Your Baby

A healthy baby is not as fragile as he may seem to you, so don't be afraid to touch, hold, rock, and cuddle him as often as possible. Even the soft spots on his head are not really soft; their sturdy membranes are designed to protect your baby's head from physical shocks, such as falling. You may even notice a pulsing of veins under the surface, but don't worry. This is normal.

## HOLDING YOUR BABY

Touching and talking to your baby leads to physical and emotional security. Holding him often is part of the bonding that will make you both comfortable with each other, so don't worry about spoiling your child for many months yet. What follows are the best ways to hold your baby.

OPTION 1 CRADLED in your arms.

OPTION 2 WITH THE BABY'S head nestled against your shoulder while you support the back with one hand and the bottom with the other.

OPTION 3 USING THE "FOOTBALL" carry. Lay the baby along one of your arms, close to your side, and cradle the head with your hand.

## PICKING UP YOUR BABY

It's important to support your baby's head when you're picking him up and laying him down during the early months. Until the third or fourth month, his neck is too weak and his head is too heavy to hold steady by himself. If you're gradual and gentle in your movements, you're also less likely to startle him unnecessarily.

**IF HE'S LYING ON HIS BACK:** (OPTION 1) Slide one hand under his neck and fan out your fingers to support his head. Bend down so that you can comfortably slide your other arm under him. Lift slowly in a compact bundle. Don't let his arms and legs dangle.

**IF HE'S LYING ON HIS STOMACH:** (OPTION 2) It may be easiest to simply roll your baby over gently on his back and pick him up as directed in option one. To pick him up directly while he lays on his stomach, put one arm under his shoulder and neck. Support his head with your hand. Slide your other arm under his middle and fan your fingers to support his trunk and thighs. Lift him slowly in a compact bundle.

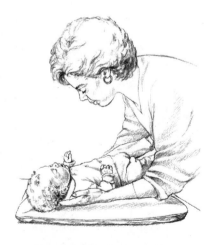

**TO PUT YOUR BABY DOWN:** Lower his head and back to the mattress while keeping your arms under him. Be especially careful to support his head as you lower it. Lower his bottom, then gently slide both your arms from underneath his body.

*A note about your baby's position*: Though it's okay to put an infant in the above positions during the waking, supervised hours, the American Academy of Pediatrics has recommended that most babies be put to sleep on their backs or sides. (See pages 37–38.)

## SWADDLING AND ROCKING

For the first several weeks of life, most babies like being firmly wrapped in a receiving blanket or shawl. Swaddling provides warmth and the sensation of constant touch. It helps quiet a baby for sleep. It's a particularly good way to soothe a "colicky" infant (see page 127), especially when you combine it with rocking.

Rocking recreates the motion your baby felt during his prenatal state. Don't rock too slowly, however. About sixty rocks per minute is a good rhythm.

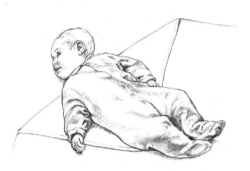

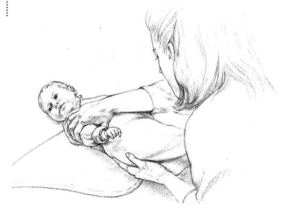

**1** SET a square blanket in front of you in a diamond shape, with a point at the top. Fold down the top point. Lay your baby on his back on the blanket so that his head is just above the edge you've folded down.

**2** TAKE UP one of the side points of the blanket, pull it firmly over the baby's chest, and tuck it under his thighs. Then bring the bottom point up over his feet.

**3** TAKE UP the other side and stretch it over the baby in the opposite direction. Tuck it under his thighs. Early on, you'll probably want to confine his arms, but later you'll want to make sure his fingers are free for sucking. Babies usually like being swaddled for the first several weeks of life and eventually will prefer to move about freely.

*A note about shaking your baby*: A baby who is held and shaken so that the neck jerks back and forth rapidly can be seriously injured. The motion can break blood vessels and cause irreversible nervous system damage. If you ever feel angry or frustrated with your baby, **never** shake him. Take a deep breath and count to ten, or ask your spouse, friend, or relative to take over so you can have a chance to regain control.

# Elimination

Changing diapers will probably never be your favorite activity. Diapers will leak, and clothing will be soiled. You may even get wet from time to time when your baby urinates in the middle of a diaper change. Try to keep your humor about it. Don't make your child feel that he has done something distasteful when he urinates or has a bowel movement, and try to avoid making comments like "yuck." He has no control over either the frequency or the manner of movements and won't for a couple of years.

## URINATION

### The First Weeks

Don't be surprised if your newborn always seems to have a wet diaper. It's normal for a newborn to urinate even up to thirty times a day. A newborn infant who stays dry for four to six hours may be dehydrated (see page 136) or have a urinary obstruction (see page 155), and should be taken to the doctor.

### The First Year

Once your baby is older, he should have at least six to eight wet diapers a day. If he has fewer, make sure he's getting enough liquid. In especially hot weather, it's okay to supplement his breast milk or formula with water or unsweetened fruit juice. If the problem persists, see a doctor.

## BOWEL MOVEMENTS

### Right after Birth

A greenish-black tar-like substance called *meconium* builds up in a baby's intestines before he is born. After birth, it must be passed out before normal digestion can occur. Generally, the intestines become free of meconium by the second or third day of your baby's life. If your child fails to eliminate the meconium by the third day,

consult your doctor or health care provider. His bowels may be obstructed.

### The Early Weeks

As your baby adjusts to getting his nourishment from the breast or bottle (rather than from the mother's placenta) his digestive system will need some time to adapt. At first, stools will probably be very frequent—occurring after every feeding or even more often—and have a loose, curd-like texture. The color may vary, and the fecal matter may be expelled quite violently. These are all normal features of your baby's early days. Despite the looseness, none of them suggests your baby has diarrhea, as long as he seems content and is feeding well. (See page 138 for more on diarrhea.) By the time he's three weeks old, his stools will take on predictable characteristics, and his movements will be less frequent.

### The First Year

- *The breast-fed baby.* The stools of a breast-fed baby are mild smelling, mustard yellow, and loose. Greenish or brownish stools or movements with a seedy or watery consistency are not uncommon and are no sign of an intestinal disturbance as long as your baby seems otherwise content. Because breast milk is so perfectly suited to your baby, it's almost impossible for him to become constipated as long as your milk is his sole source of nutrition. (See page 130 for more on constipation.) After the first few months, don't worry if your baby goes for several days without a bowel movement. Even if he does strain a bit when he finally passes one, the texture should still be soft. A frequency rate ranging from several a day to one every several days is considered normal. And it's normal for him to adjust his pattern often. As long as he's thriving, don't worry.

- *The bottle-fed baby.* The stools of a bottle-fed baby are generally more solid than those of a breast-fed baby because there is more waste for him to get rid of. They tend to be light brown or golden and are likely to smell more like ordinary adult stools. The bottle-fed baby can have as many as six movements a day in his early weeks, but then as few as one a day (and sometimes one every few days) as he matures. The important thing to watch is the consistency. In the unlikely event that his formula is not perfectly suited to him, the first sign of this may appear in his stools.

- *When solids are introduced.* Introducing anything new to your baby's digestive system may cause a change in the appearance or the smell of his stools. They may take on the actual color of any new solid food you give your baby—orange after eating carrots, for example. Some undigested food may be present in older infants.

# Diapers and Other Necessities

## DISPOSABLE DIAPERS

Disposable diapers have a plastic outer liner to keep moisture in, an inner layer of absorbent paper, and sometimes an inner plastic lining or gel that keeps moisture away from your baby's skin. Disposables come equipped with adhesive fasteners, and some brands have elastic around the legs to further prevent leaks. Have lots on hand to start with, because you'll probably use seventy to ninety diapers a week with a newborn.

## CLOTH DIAPERS

Cloth diapers are usually made out of gauze or cotton flannel. In the past, they required pins to fasten them, but they come more often now with Velcro fasteners and an outer, waterproof lining. Cloth diapers are generally quick to dry and very absorbent, and they come unfolded and prefolded. You'll probably need three or four dozen to start with if you don't use a diaper service.

- Unfolded diapers can be folded into any shape or size. This allows them to "grow" with the baby.

- Prefolded diapers come with an extra thickness down the center for added absorbency, so they don't need to be folded. This saves time but also makes them less flexible in size.

## WATERPROOF PANTS

Plastic pants have elastic around the waist and legs to prevent leakage. They allow no drying or air circulation; therefore, they can sometimes lead to diaper rash or sensitive skin. More breathable alternatives to traditional plastic pants are now available, and many diapers have outer linings sewn on. If you plan to use waterproof pants, have three or four small pairs on hand for your newborn.

## CHANGING TABLE

Any waist-high surface will work as a changing table. Various commercial changing tables are available, or you can convert an old dresser into a perfectly usable surface. Just make sure that it's covered with something soft. A foam pad or a baby carriage mattress works well. Cover the padding with a removable and washable flannel cloth. For additional protection, you may want to keep a small square of cotton-covered rubber sheeting under your baby's bottom during changing time. Put up a shelf nearby so everything you need will be within reach. It's also wise to attach a strap to the table. You'll want that extra measure of safety for wiggly babies. Remember never to leave your baby alone on the changing table.

# Choosing Diaper Care

Whether you decide to buy disposable diapers, wash your own, or use a diaper service will depend on a number of factors, including your schedule, your budget, and your baby's reaction to various kinds of diapers. The chart below lists some of the advantages and disadvantages of each method.

| METHOD | ADVANTAGES | DISADVANTAGES |
|---|---|---|
| **Washing your own diapers** | • Offers the most inexpensive way of providing diapers for your baby.<br>• Offers flexibility—cotton squares can be folded and refolded to fit your baby as he grows. (However, newer diaper designs with Velcro closures may offer less flexibility in size.) | • Is time-consuming and messy. You have to soak, wash rinse, and dry diapers before they're ready for use.<br>• Can be inconvenient when you're traveling |
| **Using disposable diapers** | • Offers convenience and is especially handy for traveling and visiting.<br>• Encouraged at many day-care centers. | • Costs roughly twice as much as caring for your own diapers (for the entire time your child spends in diapers).<br>• Demands frequent trips to the store to maintain your supply.<br>• Costs rise because your baby requires larger sizes as he grows.<br>• May cause diaper rash because the plastic outer liners prevent air circulation.<br>• Disposing of human waste in the trash is illegal in some areas, so disposables may require the same rinsing as cloth diapers.<br>• Adds 6,000 to 8,000 diapers to landfills for every baby before being toilet-trained. |
| **Using diaper service** | • Saves time. Requires no rinsing.<br>• Is less expensive than using disposables.<br>• Uses special disinfectant soaps and uses less water per diaper than washing them at home.<br>• Costs do not increase as your baby gets bigger. | • Is more expensive than washing your own diapers.<br>• Is inconvenient when you're away from home.<br>• May be hard to locate a service in some areas. |

*Note:* Despite the belief that disposable diapers prevent bacteria from spreading in day-care centers, recent research has shown that cloth and disposable diapers are equally effective in this area.

# Diaper Care

Generally speaking, cloth diapers only require special care if you wash your own. Most diaper services have special sterilizing agents on the diapers that require you only to drop soiled ones in a special pail. This feature makes using a diaper service as easy as working with disposable diapers.

## SOAKING CLOTH DIAPERS

To soak dirty cloth diapers properly, you'll need a covered, deodorized diaper pail and a soaking bleach or diaper sterilizer. Partially fill the diaper pail with water and a half to a full cup (125 to 250 ml) of soaking bleach or diaper sterilizer according to measurement instructions on the package). Then, as you remove a dirty diaper from your baby, here's what to do:

- If the diaper is simply wet, it's a good idea to rinse it first, then wring it out and drop it in the diaper pail.

- If the diaper is soiled, scrape, shake, or scrub the stool into the toilet and then rinse the diaper in the toilet or sink until the stain is well faded. Then drop the diaper into the pail.

It's best to soak your diapers in the disinfecting solution for at least six hours before you wash them. If you plan to wash diapers but have a few that haven't soaked for six hours, keep them in a plastic bag and simply add them to the next pail-full.

## WASHING AND DRYING CLOTH DIAPERS

When you are ready to wash diapers, put them in a sink and let the soaking solution drain from them before you put them in the washing machine. Another option is to put the diapers in your washing machine and run the spin cycle to drain out the soaking solution. Then add soap and begin the wash cycle.

Wash diapers with a mild soap in a machine on the hottest cycle possible with at least two rinses. If your baby suffers from diaper rash or has very sensitive skin, you may need to run an extra rinse cycle. (You can also throw plastic pants in a washing machine, but they should not go in the dryer.)

Either tumble-dry or line-dry your diapers. If you use a dryer, be aware that the scented paper squares that eliminate static or soften fabrics contain chemicals that might irritate sensitive skin. If you dry your diapers on the line but can't do it outside, they may become stiff. You'll then have to use a fabric softener in the washer's rinse cycle, but be sure it's rinsed out completely so it doesn't irritate your baby's skin.

## DISPOSABLE DIAPERS

The great convenience of disposable diapers, of course, is that you usually can just throw them away when they're dirty or wet. You should know, however, that the inner absorbent material of a disposable, which holds most of the urine or stool, is biodegradable and can be flushed down the toilet. Do not flush the inner plastic lining or the waterproof outer layer.

# Diapering Your Baby

- It's best to change your baby after every bowel movement and whenever he becomes fairly wet. This usually adds up to ten to twelve changes a day. You don't have to be obsessive, however. Because babies urinate a lot, you'll drive yourself crazy if you try to keep up.

- Unless he has an especially bad case of diaper rash, you don't need to change your baby's diapers during the night. If he's sleeping peacefully, you can be sure he's comfortable. He won't be chilled if he's covered and the wet diapers aren't exposed to air.

- See page 137 for how to treat diaper rash.

- Keep your hands dry and oil-free when you are using disposables. Otherwise, the plastic tabs might not stick. If the tabs don't stick, use masking tape to secure the diaper.

- If your baby wets a great deal at night while he's asleep, or if you don't want to rouse him for a change after a drowsy, middle-of-the-night feeding, double-diaper him before his last evening feeding, using two cloth diapers in place of one.

- If your baby's navel hasn't yet healed, fold the front edge of the diaper below the navel so it can't chafe and irritate that tender area.

- Don't turn your back on your baby when he's on the changing table. Even a newborn can wiggle and fall to the floor.

- Diapers with waterproof outer layer
- Cotton balls or washcloth
- Warm water
- Diaper rash ointment (See page 137.)
- Commercial baby wipes, which are convenient but expensive, are fine to use as long as your baby has no reaction to them.

# Step-by-Step

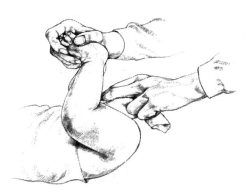

**1** PLACE YOUR BABY on his back on a changing table or other convenient, flat surface. Unfasten the used diaper and remove it. If the diaper is soiled, roll it up. With the unsoiled end of the diaper, clean any clinging stool off your baby's bottom.

**2** HOLDING YOUR BABY'S LEGS, lift his bottom up and finish the cleaning with a warm washcloth or baby wipe, always wiping from front to back. If the diaper was simply wet, you need not wash your baby. Then always allow your baby's bottom to air dry. Apply a general purpose ointment or lotion if he has diaper rash.

**3** LIFT HIS BOTTOM up again and place the fresh diaper (cloth or disposable) beneath, with the top edge of the diaper at waist level. Make sure any extending tabs —tape or Velcro—are behind your baby. Fold over any extra cloth in front for a boy or in back for a girl.

**4** BRING THE TABBED PORTIONS (for disposable or Velcro adhesive diapers) of the rectangle up over the baby's front. Then fasten the diaper securely at each side. The back should overlap the front. If you're using pins with cloth diapers, be sure to put your own hand between the diaper and your baby's skin to avoid sticking him.

# Bathing Your Baby
## (sponge baths)

- Doctors and nurses generally recommend that you give your baby sponge baths until the umbilical cord has fallen off and the navel has fully healed. If your child has been circumcised, sponge bathe him until his penis has fully healed. (The circumcision usually heals before the cord falls off.)

- You need not bathe or shampoo your child every day. Two or three times a week is often enough as long as you keep his face and genital area clean. More frequent shampoos could cause a dry, scaly scalp.

- Newborns sometimes fear being completely naked, so if your baby seems annoyed during his bath, you might try uncovering and washing only one part of him at a time.

- Some babies don't like to lie still or stay quiet long enough for a complete sponge bath, so you can do it one step at a time at intervals throughout the day—for instance, each time you change him.

- A bowl of warm water
- A soft washcloth
- Cotton balls
- Gentle, unscented soap
- A soft towel
- Cotton swabs
- Rubbing alcohol
- A sponge cushion (optional)

# Step-by-Step

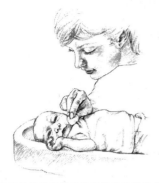

**1** WITHOUT UNDRESSING your baby, place him on a sponge cushion or a changing table. Starting with his head, wipe each eye with a separate clean cotton ball moistened with warm water. Wipe from the inside of the eye outward. With another moistened cotton ball, wipe around your baby's ears. Continue with a damp cloth to clean around his mouth, chin, and neck.

**2** HOLD your baby's head over a bowl of water and gently wet his scalp. Then shampoo it with a mild soap, making sure you massage it gently with your fingertips, not your fingernails. Rinse his head and pat it dry.

**3** REMOVE his shirt and gently wash his chest and arms, making sure you get at all the creases in his skin, including those around his neck and under his arms. Wipe his hands and check for lint between his fingers. Also look for long or sharp fingernails. (See page 35 for how to trim fingernails.) Rinse him with clean, warm water and pat dry. Lift his bottom up again and place the fresh diaper (cloth or disposable) beneath, with the top edge of the diaper at waist level. Make sure any extending tabs—tape or Velcro—are behind your baby. Fold over any extra cloth in front for a boy or in back for a girl.

**4** WHILE SUPPORTING his head, gently turn your baby on his side and wash and rinse his back. Pat dry and dress his top half.

**5** WHILE IT'S STILL HEALING, wipe the navel with a cotton swab soaked in rubbing alcohol. Clean it right down to the base. Avoid wetting the navel area until it has completely healed.

# Bathing Your Baby
## (tub baths—small tubs)

**TIPS**

- It is generally advised that you don't bathe your baby in a tub until the umbilical cord has fallen off and the navel has fully healed. If your child has been circumcised, wait until his penis has completely healed before giving a tub bath.

- As noted earlier, you need not bathe or shampoo your child every day. Two or three times a week is often enough as long as you keep his face and genital area clean.

- It is safest to use a mild, unscented soap. Any disinfectant or highly perfumed soap may be irritating to the skin and cause dryness and rashes.

- Your baby may not initially like a full bath. Don't worry and don't force him. Continue giving him sponge baths until he's a little older, and remember that most babies eventually have a great time in their baths. Don't rush; you'll both soon be enjoying it.

- You should never turn your back on your baby or leave him alone in the tub, no matter how short a time and how little water you're using. If you must leave him to answer the phone, quickly wrap him in a towel and put him on the floor.

**MATERIALS**

- A portable baby tub with sponge cushion (a plastic dish tub will work for a smaller baby)

- A table or counter top at a convenient height

- A soft washcloth

- Soft, unscented soap

- A soft towel

- Baby shampoo

- You can also bathe your baby in the kitchen sink so long as you can rotate the spigot away from the sink to prevent injury.

# Step-by-Step

**1** RUN about two inches (5 cm) of water in the tub and then check the water temperature to make sure it's pleasantly warm. Extreme temperatures can scald, burn, or shock an infant. Gently lower the baby into the tub by easing his bottom in first.

**2** USING a soft washcloth and gentle soap, start by washing your baby's face, ears, and neck. Work your way down, paying attention to folds in the neck and lint between the fingers and toes, just as you would with a sponge bath. (See page 31.) Rinse well.

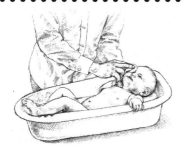

**3** SUPPORT your baby in a reclining position and shampoo his head by working from front to back so that the soap doesn't get into his eyes. Scrub the scalp well, using the tips of your fingers. Don't worry about the soft spot on his head; it's tough. After you've rinsed, pat (don't rub) your baby dry.

# Bathing Your Baby (tub baths—the big tub)

TIPS

- Your child is probably ready for bathing in a standard bathtub by the time he's able to sit up steadily unsupported, and certainly by the time he's too big for his infant tub.

- To eliminate the risk of a possible drowning or even an unintentional dunking, be sure to run only a few inches of water in the tub for your baby's bath. Never leave your baby unattended in the bath.

- Always test the bath water before you put your baby in. It should be mildly warm to the touch. Try to keep your child away from the faucets during the bath; one playful turn of the hot water and he could scald himself. Run a little cold water last so that if your child touches the faucet, it won't burn him.

- At first you may want to bathe with your child to make sure he doesn't slip and bump himself. This also saves you the trouble of kneeling on a hard tile floor and bending over throughout his bath. You can also place no-slip strips on the bottom of the tub to help prevent falls. In any event, you shouldn't let your baby stand in the tub (once he's able to) without keeping one hand on him all the time.

# Skin Care

Bathing with water and a mild, unscented soap and then rinsing the skin thoroughly is all the skin care your baby is likely to need. Some parents apply powders and lotions to make their babies smell good and to keep their skin from drying out or chafing. The best way to avoid dry skin, however, is not to bathe your baby too often. Use skin-care products sparingly and note the following cautions:

*Baby powders and cornstarch.* Neither is necessary for your baby's skin, and some evidence even suggests that cornstarch creates a breeding ground for some of the infections that cause diaper rash. If you do use these products, do so cautiously so you don't create a cloud of powder that the baby might breathe. Shake the powder into your hand as far away from the baby's face as possible. (Avoid using zinc stearate powders because they irritate the lungs.) Apply any powder or cornstarch lightly to avoid caking it on your baby's skin.

*Baby lotions and oils.* These products are not needed either, but your baby may love it if you gently massage him with a little lotion or oil after his bath. (See next page.) Be cautious if you're using mineral oils, because they can cause a rash on some babies.

## THE NAVEL

The stump of the umbilical cord, which remains temporarily attached to the navel, should be kept clean, dry, and free from diaper irritation. After each bath and diaper change, swab it with a sterile cotton ball or cotton-tipped swab dipped in rubbing alcohol. When you're putting diapers on your infant, fold the front edge below the healing navel so it doesn't rub against that area. You don't need to put a sterile dressing on a navel that's healing normally.

The stump usually will fall off between ten and fourteen days after birth. Even after it has fallen off, continue to clean the navel with alcohol. Keep it dry, and watch it carefully until it completely heals over. After the stump has fallen off, there may be a little secretion or pinkish discharge from the navel. This is normal. However, you should report any bloody discharge that continues for more than a week, any profuse bleeding, or any red swelling around a healing navel to your health care provider. Also, if the cord remains on longer than three weeks, mention this to your health care provider at the next checkup.

## THE PENIS

- *Circumcised.* Until the circumcised penis is healed—usually by three to ten days after the operation—treat the tip with petroleum jelly after each diaper change and after a bath. The jelly will protect it against diaper irritation and encourage healing.

  While the penis is healing, it is not uncommon for the wound to secrete a few drops of blood. This is normal and no cause for alarm. It is also normal for a healing penis to get a white or gray-yellow coating on the tip. Once the circumcised penis heals, usually the only care it needs is normal washing. But if some of the foreskin remains, you should pull it back gently when diapering or bathing.

- *Uncircumcised.* The uncircumcised penis requires no special care. Wash it with warm, soapy water and rinse the area just as you would any other part of his body. When your boy is very young, you'll probably find it impossible to retract his foreskin. As he gets older, however, you'll find that his foreskin will separate naturally. But it may not retract completely until sometime in adolescence.

## BABY MASSAGE

Babies are especially sensitive to touch, so your infant may find a light, gentle massage extremely soothing and comforting. You can improvise by rubbing a little lotion or oil into your baby's skin after his bath. You can even warm up the oil by setting it in his bath water. Starting with his neck, slowly, gently, and rhythmically work your way down to his feet. Don't forget his arms and hands. Then turn him over and massage his shoulders, back, and buttocks. Finally, beginning with the forehead and working down, massage his face.

## TRIMMING FINGERNAILS

When your baby is newborn, keeping his fingernails short is important for his own protection. During his finger play, he could easily scratch his face if his nails are not short and smoothly cut. As your child grows older, trimmed nails are for your protection. He'll delight in exploring your face with his hands, and long or ragged nails could unintentionally scratch you. At all times, short fingernails are a sensible hygienic measure for your baby. Dirt collects under his nails, and it'll be years before he quits putting his fingers in his mouth.

Here's what to do when you cut your baby's nails:

- Be sure to use blunt-tipped fingernail scissors. Even the most docile, sleepy infant can make a sudden move that may cause you to poke him if you're using pointed scissors.

- Trim the fingernails (or toenails) when your baby is asleep or after a bath, when his nails are softer and easier to cut.

- Cut fingernails and toenails straight across. Make sure you leave no ragged edges.

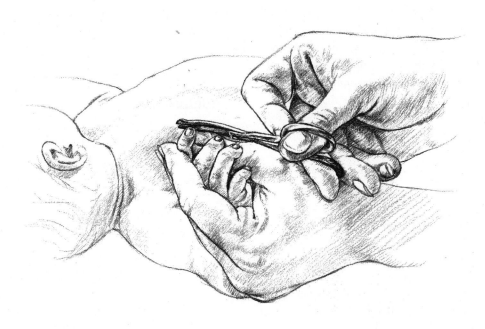

# Sleeping

Sleep—your own and your baby's—will probably be on your mind frequently throughout your child's first year of life. New parents find themselves talking with anyone who will listen about the length and frequency of their baby's sleep patterns. It can't be helped. Getting by on less sleep each night is one of the biggest adjustments you have to make as a new parent, and although your chances of getting an uninterrupted night's rest increase as your baby gets older, a few years may pass before your sleep life is back to what it was before you had a child.

As in many other things, babies vary in their sleep needs and habits. Your newborn may sleep for twenty-two hours a day or may get by on twelve. If he's healthy, he's probably getting enough sleep, even if it seems too much or too little to you. You may be somewhat surprised by the nature of his sleep at this stage. Three kinds of sleep seem to characterize the early period: quiet sleep, which seems deep and calm; active sleep, which is accompanied by sucking, grimacing, and rapid eye movements; and drifting sleep, during which your baby drowsily floats in and out of sleep. It's probably impossible for new parents not to check on their newborn at night, but don't be too alarmed at the snuffling noises and sometimes fretful sounds he makes. They're normal.

As he gets older, your baby may settle into a pattern of taking one or two good naps during the day and then sleeping for a solid stretch of time at night. (How long a stretch is another issue. See sleeping through the night, page 39.) By the end of his first year, he may even give up one of those naps. Happily, the older your baby gets, the more active he'll become during the day, especially when he starts crawling and then walking. The more energy he expends during the day, the easier he may fall asleep at night.

## BASIC EQUIPMENT

A newborn doesn't need a crib. You can start him out in a bassinet, a cradle, a lined basket, or even a padded drawer or sturdy cardboard box. Just make sure the sides are high enough to prevent him from rolling out. As he gets older and bigger, you'll most likely want to move him to a crib. (See page 84 for what to look for in a crib.) Whether he sleeps in a bassinet or a crib, you'll want to make sure that you do the following:

- Use a firm, nonallergenic mattress, because a soft mattress can suffocate a baby. (An inner-spring mattress will hold its shape longer than a foam mattress.)

- Put a waterproof cover on the mattress, and stretch a fitted sheet on top of that.

- Line the sides of the bed with bumpers or soft, washable fabric.

- Don't use a pillow, which could smother a newborn.

## SURROUNDINGS

- Although a newborn can sleep anywhere, it is probably a good idea, especially at night, to begin a routine of putting your baby to sleep in a separate room. That way, you won't be distracted at night by his restless periods, and he will gradually come to associate a particular place with sleep time.

- Try to keep the temperature of your baby's room around 70°F (21.1°C) if you can. During the winter, though, if you're trying to conserve energy or cut your heating bills, you can turn your thermostat down at night so long as you take care to wrap your baby in a blanket or put him in a blanket sleeper. (But don't use an electric blanket.) Also, make sure his crib is not positioned next to a cold window and is as close to the heating vent or radiator as safety permits.

- When necessary, use a cool-mist humidifier or vaporizer in winter and a fan in summer, but don't put them too close to the bed. Be sure you regularly clean the vaporizer; if you don't, it can become contaminated with organisms that can spread through the air when it's on. Chlorine bleach works especially well to clean vaporizers and humidifiers, but be sure to rinse thoroughly after cleaning so your baby doesn't breathe chlorine fumes. Use the purest water you can. Otherwise the humidifier will emit contaminants from the water itself into the air.

- You don't need to hush the entire house when your baby sleeps. He'll easily get used to the normal sound levels. But try to avoid abrupt changes in the noise level, which can startle and wake him up.

- Make sure there are shades or curtains in your baby's room that you can draw to cut out sunlight during daytime naps.

- In warm weather, you can let your baby take naps outside, but don't put him in direct sunlight. Protect him against flies and mosquitoes with netting over the bassinet or carriage.

## GETTING YOUR BABY TO SLEEP

Early in his first year, your baby will probably always need a little (or a lot of) help going to sleep at night. It's difficult for a new baby to learn to shut out all the outside stimuli that he needs to before sleep is possible. It's a rare baby who, after being put in his crib and kissed good-night, will drift off to sleep without protest. You'll often need to soothe and quiet him first. The best way to soothe him is often to nurse him or give him a bottle. If he's not hungry, you can also try the following ideas:

- Swaddle or rock him until he falls asleep. After about four months of age, it's a good idea to set the baby in the crib before he is completely asleep, so he learns that he can settle himself.

- Car rides, carriage rides, swings, and the rhythm of your walk as you hold him will often lull an excited baby to sleep.

- Use soft, rhythmical background noise. It need not be music; the monotonous drone of a fan, vaporizer, dish washer, or air conditioner will work. Or you might try playing a recorded heartbeat over and over. If you start right after birth, a heartbeat may be a soothing reminder of his prenatal state. Several companies have recorded lullaby tapes with the sound of a heartbeat underneath. Some even have a baby blanket with a special pouch to hold the heartbeat tape.

- Put your baby across your lap and give him a gentle back rub.

- Fresh air seems to make babies sleepy. Take him outside or put his bed near an open window if it's not too cold.

## SLEEP POSITIONS

The American Academy of Pediatrics Task Force on Infant Positioning and Sudden Infant Death Syndrome (SIDS) recommends that all healthy infants be placed on their sides or backs, not their stomachs when being put down for sleep. Studies from other countries indicate a decrease in the incidence of SIDS when infants are on their sides or backs. The actual risk for SIDS, even in babies placed on their stomachs, is extremely low.

This said, some babies with certain medical conditions should be placed on their stomachs to sleep. These babies include some babies who are premature and those who have gastroesophageal reflux or anomalies of the upper airway.

For a nap after a feeding, laying your baby on his right side will help digestion. The stomach, which is on the left side, can empty more easily into the intestinal tract, which is on the right. Don't put him on his back, however. If he spits up, he's more likely to choke. If you have questions about your baby's sleep position, talk with your health care provider.

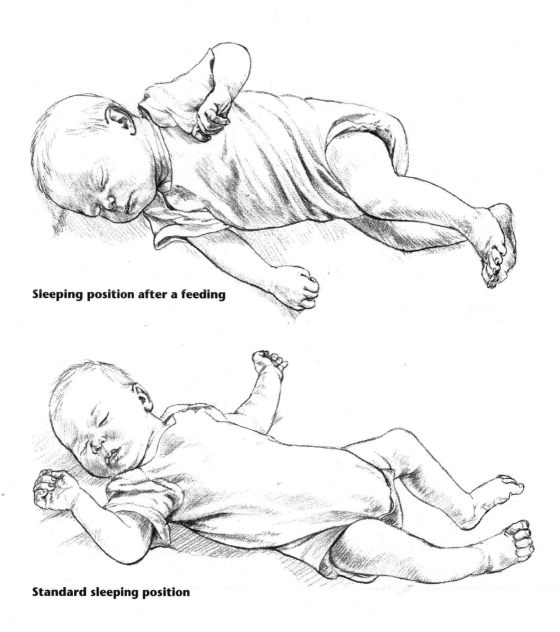

**Sleeping position after a feeding**

**Standard sleeping position**

## MIXING UP DAYS AND NIGHTS

Babies tend to get their days and nights mixed up. Some end up sleeping more during the day than at night, and that usually results in a baby who's wide awake and ready to play at 4 A.M. Here are some things you can do to reverse this:

- Treat daytime naps differently from nightly bedtime routines. During the day, let your baby take his naps anywhere in the house, but at night, put him in his own room.

- Don't let your baby sleep more than four uninterrupted hours during the day.

- Stimulate the baby more when he's awake during the day by singing or massaging him. But at night, be quiet and businesslike during feeding, and keep the room dark.

## SLEEPING THROUGH THE NIGHT

When (or even whether) your baby starts to sleep through the night during his first year is one of the issues new parents are often passionately concerned about. As a new parent, you'll probably hear about babies who have slept through the night since they were three months—or even three weeks—old, and you'll wonder why your child is still getting up twice a night at six months. Not much can be gained by these kinds of comparisons except frustration, so don't let them worry you too much.

Actually, very few babies will really sleep through the night without waking up during their first year of life. In a recent study of night-waking in infants, less than 20 percent of a group of nine-month-olds slept without waking at least once between midnight and 5 A.M. Another survey suggests that breast-fed babies are more prone to wake up during the night than bottle-fed babies.

The vexing question that parents have to face is really rather simple: If I'm sure that my baby is neither hungry nor sick, what should I do when he wakes up at night? Though the question is simple, the answers are not. Even the experts disagree on the best way to handle night-waking.

Some parents cannot bear to hear their infants cry at night. They reason that a crying infant must have some need that could be satisfied, and that it's best for the child if the parent attends to him promptly and tries to soothe him back to sleep. That way both the parent and the infant get back to sleep as soon as possible. By the second half of your child's first year, however, your reactions may reinforce this behavior in your child and create the expectation that you will always come when he wakes up at night.

Other parents, hoping that the infants will cry themselves back to sleep, try to leave their infants alone. This can be difficult, because it may mean listening to your baby cry for fifteen to twenty minutes each time he wakes. However, it is often the fastest means for eventually getting your baby to sleep through the night. You may need to talk with other parents and your physician before you decide how to handle this issue. The important thing is that you do something you feel comfortable with. Babies have different temperaments, and no single solution will work for everyone.

# Comforting a Crying Baby

All babies cry, of course, and one of your first challenges as a new parent will be to figure out why and to learn how you can make it stop. You can comfort your baby most of the time by satisfying one of his basic needs—food, a changed diaper, sleep, entertainment. But most babies seem to go through a fussy period each day when nothing seems to work but letting them cry it out. The following paragraphs offer some suggestions about how to comfort a crying infant.

## HUNGER

Most of the time a baby who is crying is hungry, and the obvious solution is to feed him.

## GAS IN STOMACH

To burp your baby, use one of the techniques described on pages 68–69. Some babies need one burp for every three to five minutes of feeding time. Some babies are delayed burpers, meaning they may go for a half hour between the end of their feeding and their first burp. Just keep trying.

## NEED TO SUCK

Most babies are born with an intense sucking reflex. Sucking is not only a means of nourishment, but it also soothes and comforts them. If you're nursing your child, the breast is the best possible source of comfort, but if he's clearly not hungry, you can offer him a pacifier or help him find his thumb or fingers for sucking.

## WET DIAPERS

Change your baby's diapers if they're wet or soiled. The average newborn needs ten to twelve diapers per day. Even if changing your infant's diapers doesn't seem to do the trick, at least by changing him you haven't contributed to the potential problem of diaper rash.

## TEMPERATURE EXTREMES

If your baby is too warm or too cold, he will cry out of discomfort. Try to be sensitive to your baby's needs and be sure not to overdress him, leave him in drafts, or take him out in the cold if he's not properly bundled. A good rule of thumb is to keep your baby covered with the same amount of clothing you would need to keep yourself comfortable.

## BOREDOM

Your baby can become bored, just as you can, and his cry can be a way of requesting some stimuli. (See pages 101–108 for ways to entertain a bored baby.)

## LACK OF CONTACT

Babies, especially newborns, need a great deal of physical contact, and it is impossible to give them too much. Remember that there's nothing wrong or spoiled about a baby under four months of age who likes to be held constantly. Try to arrange your schedule so you can give him a lot of contact.

## COLIC

If nothing seems to comfort your baby, and he's less than three or four months old, it's possible he has colic. (See page 127 for more details and suggestions.)

# Thumb Sucking and Pacifiers

All babies have a need to suck, and yours may need more than breastfeeding or bottlefeeding allow. Some babies suck their thumbs and fingers even before they're born. They seem to have a natural knack for comforting themselves in this way. If your baby hasn't found his own thumb, and you don't want to introduce a pacifier, you can help him by gently guiding it into his mouth. This might quiet him when he's fussy.

According to the American Dental Association, there is little reason to fear that thumb or finger sucking will harm a baby's teeth or jaws. It shouldn't be a matter of concern unless the child is three or four years old and sucking with a great deal of pressure on the jaws. Most babies give up the habit when they're between eighteen months and two years of age. The practice may crop up infrequently after that point, especially in times of fatigue, stress, or fear, but this is natural and shouldn't be discouraged.

## PACIFIERS

A baby who has a great need to suck or who is difficult to comfort may find great relief in a pacifier, though opinions on their use vary widely. Orthodontic pacifiers on the market are designed not to interfere with the development of your child's teeth and jaws, and it's easier to wean a child from a pacifier than from a thumb. However, removing a pacifier doesn't mean a child won't suck his thumb. Here's some advice about pacifier use:

- Be careful not to pop the pacifier in your baby's mouth whenever he seems fussy. Make sure all of his basic needs, such as food, dry clothes, warmth, and cuddling are met first.

- If you let your baby have a pacifier in bed, he may begin to need it to fall asleep at night, and then wake up crying for it whenever it falls out of his mouth. This could happen several times a night. To eliminate this problem, try to remove the pacifier once your child gets sleepy.

- Never tie a pacifier around your child's neck. The string or cord could accidentally strangle him. Also, never make a homemade pacifier from a bottle nipple stuffed with cotton. Babies have been known to breathe them in and suffocate.

- Never coat a pacifier with honey. There is a possible connection between honey and infant botulism in the first year.

# Clothing and Shoes for Your Baby

## BUYING CLOTHING

Babies grow quickly during their first year of life, so don't be surprised if your infant rapidly outgrows his clothes. The average baby will double his birth weight in five to six months and triple it by the end of the year. Babies also generally grow eight inches (20 cm) during their first year.

- Some clothing comes in a newborn or three-month size, but it may be more economical for you to buy a six-month or up-to-eighteen-pounds size and allow your baby to grow into it. Check the labels for weight as well as age; you may have a child who is smaller or larger than average. The following chart is a general guide for determining your baby's size:

| WEIGHT | SIZE |
|---|---|
| Birth–13 lbs. | 3 months |
| 14–18 lbs. | 6 months |
| 19–22 lbs. | 12 months |
| 23–25 lbs. | 18 months |
| 26–28 lbs. | 24 months |
| 29–32 lbs. | 36 months |

- Many babies hate having clothes pulled over their heads. Look for shirts with side or front openings, shoulder snaps, or large, easily stretchable necklines. Buy clothing that also allows easy access to your baby's diapers for changing. Open fronts, snap crotch and legs, or pants can be removed easily.

- Look at how the clothing is made. Most baby clothes will need numerous washings. Check for well-constructed seams and sturdy zippers. Are the seams soft enough inside that they won't irritate your baby's skin?

## DRESSING YOUR BABY

Babies are able to produce heat from the time they are born. New babies, however, can't conserve the heat they make. They lose it as fast as they make it. As the baby grows, he gains more ability to conserve his own warmth and will need to expend less energy to keep warm. Here are some tips on dressing your child and keeping him at a comfortable temperature:

- In warm weather, babies are more often overdressed than underdressed. Overdressing causes rashes and excess sweating. In hot weather, your baby should wear as little clothing as possible.

- In cold weather, use layers of clothing so you'll be able to add or subtract clothing in response to the temperature inside or out. For a newborn baby, a short trip in cold weather is usually fine if he is dressed properly. But a longer trip, especially if the baby falls asleep, may cause chilling. Cheeks can get cold easily, so be careful about prolonged exposure to this area.

- The older and more active your baby gets, the more difficult it will be to keep him still while you dress him. Happily, you'll be getting more efficient at the process, but you'll probably need to rely on games and songs to keep him quiet. You might also try keeping a special toy handy to keep him diverted.

- To put on a shirt, gather the neck opening into a loop. Slip it first over the back of your baby's head, then forward. Stretch the opening as you bring it down gently past the forehead and nose so you don't scratch his face.

- To pull on sleeves, put your left hand up the sleeve and grasp your baby's hand. With your other hand, pull the sleeve over his arms.

- To take off a shirt, take your baby's arms out of the sleeves first, then stretch the neckline open. Raise the front part of the neck opening past the nose and forehead, then slip the shirt off toward the back of the head.

- To put on a blanket sleeper or stretch suit, it's often easiest to start by spreading the sleeper or suit out on the changing table or bed and then laying your baby on top of it. Slide his legs in first, then his arms, and zip or snap it up.

## SHOES AND SOCKS

Babies do not need shoes except for protection on certain surfaces and for warmth. Bare feet are fine before a baby walks and even when he starts walking inside. An infant's arches are relatively flat at first, so by using his feet he builds the arches up and strengthens his ankles. In addition, with bare feet your baby can use his toes for balance, which may be safer. When you do decide to get shoes for your baby, here are some things to keep in mind:

- A newly standing baby wearing his first shoes may find it difficult to balance. He may fall more often until he gets used to them.

- For walking on uncarpeted floors, avoid socks or booties that don't have slip-resistant soles. Socks can be very slippery.

- Take your baby along when you buy him new shoes. It's important to get a good fit. Make sure that shoes are measured for width and length. Shoes and boots should be checked for size every three months.

- Make sure you consider socks when fitting new shoes. Try shoes on with the appropriate weight sock for the season. Socks should also fit well. One that is too small can constrict your baby's toes.

- Have your baby stand or walk in the shoe to see how it fits. There should be one-half inch (1.25 cm) of space beyond the longest toe for growth.

- Baby shoes can be expensive, but don't feel you need to buy the most expensive, sturdiest shoe. As long as the shoe fits well, and your baby is comfortable wearing it, an inexpensive shoe will do fine. Tennis shoes, for instance, are perfectly appropriate for babies. They're soft, flexible, and less expensive than leather shoes. Although it's rarely necessary, have a baby with special shoe needs examined by a physician.

# Clothing Checklist

The types of clothes you'll find useful during your child's first year are listed below. These are only suggestions of course; the actual number of each item you'll need will depend on how often you do laundry, the season, your child's age, and other factors.

| ITEM | NUMBER | DESCRIPTION |
|---|---|---|
| **FOR A NEWBORN** | | |
| ____Undershirts | 4-6 | Undershirts provide extra warmth when worn under other clothing, and in the summer your baby will usually be happy wearing just an undershirt and diaper. They're available in slip-on or side-snap styles. |
| ____Gowns | 4 | These long-sleeved garments with a snap neckline and an open, closed, or drawstring bottom are good for the first few months but awkward when your baby starts to creep or crawl. You may want to get gowns with elastic to avoid the drawstring coming out and becoming a danger to your baby. |
| ____Stretch suits | 4 | These one-piece suits have front snaps that run from neck to foot, making it easy to change them. The suits can be worn day or night. Stretch material is comfortable and allows room for growth. |
| ____Blanket sleepers | 3-4 | These come in two forms: a bag that allows room for growth, or shaped like coveralls with built-in feet. They usually have a front zipper. Some babies' feet get excessively sweaty when they wear sleepers with plastic feet. |
| ____Receiving blankets | 4-6 | Soft, light blankets have many uses: for swaddling a newborn; as light cover; as surface cover for changing; and rolled up as an extra padding or crib guard in a cradle, bassinet, car seat, or infant seat. |
| ____Blankets | 2 | Knitted shawls or blankets, often made of orlon or acrylic, are warm and washable. They wrap easily and stay tucked around your baby. |

| ITEM | NUMBER | DESCRIPTION |
|---|---|---|
| ____Sweaters | 1-2 | Usually made of orlon or acrylic, sweaters are available in front- or back-opening styles. (Wool sweaters are scratchy and harder to wash, and some babies are allergic to wool.) |
| ____Booties/socks | 1-3 pr. | These are only for keeping your baby's feet warm in cooler outdoor temperatures, or in a cool house. Infant feet are naturally cool, so let the temperature inside or outside be your guide. |

**FOR AN OLDER BABY**

| ITEM | NUMBER | DESCRIPTION |
|---|---|---|
| ____Coveralls or overalls | 2-3 | Overalls are practical and comfortable for older babies who are starting to creep or crawl. The crawling baby needs extra padding for more active play, especially in knee and bottom areas. Most coveralls for young babies have snap crotch and legs for easy changing. |
| ____Shirts | 2-3 | Shirts (long and short sleeved) come in a variety of styles with crew necks and turtle necks, and with snaps or buttons down the front or on the shoulder. Make sure the shirt fits easily over your baby's head. |
| ____Dresses | — | Dresses are nice for older girls but not very practical for a small baby. They don't keep the legs warm and are often bothersome for baby and parent because they tend to bunch up. Choose shorter rather than longer styles because longer dresses tend to get in the crawling baby's way. In cooler weather, stretch tights should be worn under a dress. |
| ____Hat | 1-2 | Cotton or synthetic caps work well in the summer to protect your baby's head and face from direct sunlight. Knitted hats, usually made of orlon or wool, are useful in cooler weather when it's advisable to keep the ears and head covered. |

| ITEM | NUMBER | DESCRIPTION |
|------|--------|-------------|
| ____Snowsuits | 1 | Snowsuits are made of heavy and durable material. Many have optional snap-on mittens and hoods. Choose a suit that's a little too large, because it will have to go over clothing. Avoid slippery fabric—it's hard enough to hold a wiggly baby. |
| ____Bunting | 1 | A bunting is a bag made of soft, heavy fabric—often quilted or lined—and usually has a front zipper. It's good for outings in cooler weather and allows your baby room to move and grow. Not an essential item. |

# Finding a Day-Care Provider

Many parents find that they must look beyond themselves for others to participate in the care of their babies. Parents' needs range from those who work full-time away from home to those who need a few hours each week for chores or just to get away.

There are many possible arrangements you can make for child care. The most important consideration is finding a nurturing and safe environment, regardless of whether it is in a home or in a day-care center. The care should be tailored to meet your infant's developmental stage, personality, and special needs.

Until around seven months of age, infants are often very open to care from other providers and not so fearful of separating from their parents. Later in the first year, infants are likely to protest more, and it's wise to accompany your child to a new environment and stay with him for a while.

## WHAT TO LOOK FOR

You should not rely on the telephone and references alone when you search for a day-care center or individual to watch over your child. It's best to visit a potential center in person—and more than once—so you can find a consistently safe and friendly environment. Here are some more tips to keep in mind:

- Make sure there is one caregiver for every two to three babies. A consistent caregiver will make your infant more comfortable as a familiar relationship develops.

- Find a caregiver who is stimulating and learns the ways different babies communicate.

- Observe both the cleanliness of the setting as well as the availability of safe, colorful toys, books, and interactive games. Caregivers should wash their hands often, especially after every diaper change.

- Ensure that there is a supervised, quiet space where your baby can take a nap or rest. (See pages 83–87 for safety guidelines on baby equipment.)

- Check the outside play area to see that it is safe and supervised, without any ditches, hard surfaces, or access to the street.

- See that inside space is large enough for the number of children present (thirty-five clear square feet per child) and that the noise level is comfortable.

- Ask yourself if the children seem well cared for, comfortable, clean, and free to interact with each other.

## WHAT TO ASK

- Does the provider serve meals? See menus and snack foods to make sure they are nutritious.

- Does the provider allow you to visit and observe at any time?

- Is the center or home licensed or registered with the local government? Ask for documentation.

- What is the daily plan for activities, naps, and meals? Check to see that any television viewing is limited and appropriate.

- Is there a written policy on discipline? Ask to see it.

- Can caregivers smoke around the children?

- What is the policy on ill children coming to the facility or home? Are there provisions for infants who become ill during the day?

# CHAPTER 3

# Feeding Your Baby

Some of the deepest joys of early parenting are in store when you feed your baby. Nothing can compete with the beauty of your blissful, weeks-old infant contentedly sucking at the breast or bottle and gradually easing off to sleep. No more cherished sensation exists than the feeling of your own child, nestled warm and relaxed in your arms, receiving from you the nourishment that she vitally needs.

How to provide this nourishment is the subject of this chapter. A baby will grow more during her first year than at any other time in her life. A baby's weight will generally triple by the first birthday, and the length will typically grow eight inches (20 cm). (See the weight and length charts on pages 164–165.) What your baby takes in nutritionally has a great deal to do with how well your baby grows.

Not surprisingly, then, most parents give serious thought to the question of how they're going to feed their newborn—with breast milk or formula. It's not a decision you can put off making: you'll need to decide before your baby is born. Each option requires some preparation and special equipment.

The American Academy of Pediatrics recommends that mothers breast-feed their infants, because no formula can rival breast milk, which is perfectly compatible with a baby's needs. Nor can a bottle exactly imitate the sensation of the breast. But there are advantages to both methods of feeding (see page 50), so you'll need to look closely at your own special circumstances in order to decide. Remember: Happy, healthy, and well-adjusted babies have been brought up on each method.

When your infant is about six months old, she'll be ready to start eating solids, and your concern over her getting a balanced diet will increase. Once she starts making her personal likes and dislikes known, as she will when she has the opportunity to choose between apples and peas—or nothing at all—your control starts to diminish. Your baby's own personal style also emerges. She may be an easygoing eater, a vigorous masher, an energetic thrower, or a combination of all types, depending on the time of day, her mood, or who knows what!

But eating solid foods also presents a major milestone in your baby's first year. It's just part of the inevitable road to independence.

# Breastfeeding and Bottlefeeding

## ADVANTAGES OF BREASTFEEDING

- Breast milk is nature's milk, and formulas can't duplicate it perfectly. The composition of breast milk is ideally suited to the nutritional needs of a newborn.

- Before the actual milk comes in, a mother's breasts produce colostrum, a yellowish, watery fluid that contains important antibodies and the proper nourishment for a newborn baby.

- Breastfeeding provides immunities that help keep the breast-fed infant from getting sick. Breast-fed babies also experience fewer allergies.

- You're less likely to overfeed a breast-fed baby, who will just stop nursing when she's full. There's no need to worry about your baby gaining too much weight. Bottlefeeding, on the other hand, can encourage a baby to finish a bottle, even if it is more than what's needed.

- Breastfeeding your child is convenient, economical, and time-saving. You don't have to bother with bottles and formula. Traveling with a breast-fed baby is simple, because you don't have bags of equipment to carry around.

- The stools of a breast-fed infant are mild smelling and inoffensive to clean up, and breast-fed babies are less likely to have diarrhea.

- Breastfeeding is a pleasant way to provide the warm, human contact that is so important in early infant development, and it's a very good way to satisfy the strong sucking urge that babies have.

- Because making breast milk uses up the mother's calories—about five hundred per day—and because breastfeeding causes the uterus to contract quickly to its pre-pregnancy size, a nursing mother will generally regain her figure faster than a mother who is bottlefeeding her child.

## ADVANTAGES OF BOTTLEFEEDING

- The mother of a bottle-fed baby is not the child's sole source of sustenance. Other people can easily feed the child if she decides to go back to work or out for an afternoon.

- Bottlefeeding allows a baby's father to take an active part in feeding and take equal responsibility for the nighttime feedings, thus letting a postpartum mother get a few extra hours of much-needed sleep.

- The mother of a bottle-fed baby doesn't have to worry about how her breast milk will be affected by what she eats or drinks, what medications she takes, and how much rest she gets.

- Parents of a bottle-fed baby know exactly how much milk their infant is consuming.

- In public, bottlefeeding may be more comfortable for those women who would feel a need for privacy while breastfeeding.

- Because formula takes longer to digest than breast milk, feedings may be more spread out.

# Breastfeeding Basics

## PREPARATIONS

If you plan to breast-feed your child, it helps to have a positive attitude and seek support systems that will help you initiate and maintain successful nursing. Physically, your body will be preparing your breast on its own for the lactation process. Early in pregnancy the areola, the base area of the nipple, darkens. The breasts enlarge, and the body stores some extra fat throughout for energy. After at least sixteen weeks, a thin, rich fluid called colostrum can be expressed by squeezing the areola.

Here are some physical things you should know about preparing to breast-feed:

- Wash your nipples with water only, not soap, which can remove the natural protection of the skin's own oils.

- You need not toughen your nipples, as was previously thought. In fact, overly aggressive manipulation may harm the tiny glands in the areola and in late pregnancy could release a hormone that brings about uterus contractions. You need not worry, however, about gentle stimulation (as a part of love-making, for example).

- Lotions and ointments are unnecessary and can clog skin pores, cause irritation, or be absorbed.

- A well-fitted bra can help prevent future sagging. You can even wear nursing bras, which are often adjustable, before delivery.

- If you have had recent breast cancer or surgery, especially one that reduced the size of the breasts and/or involved nipple transplantation, you should consult a specialist or your surgeon about whether you can breast-feed.

- If your nipples are inverted, you can still breast-feed a baby. Discuss this with your health care provider, because you can take several steps during your pregnancy to prepare your nipples. In many cases, a plastic device called a breast shield, worn inside a bra, will create gentle pressure on the areola, thus causing the nipple to evert more.

## SIZE OF BREASTS

The size of your breasts has absolutely nothing to do with your ability to nurse. Milk is produced in glands deep within the chest and is in no way influenced by the amount of surface fat that makes up the visible breast.

## FIRST MILK

Milk commonly comes in from two to six days after birth—on the late side if the baby is the mother's first, and on the early side if she has previously given birth.

## COLOSTRUM

What a nursing baby will receive during her first nursing sessions, before the actual milk comes in, is called colostrum. This watery, yellowish substance is high in nourishing proteins and full of immunities that protect babies from harmful infections. Your baby's need for colostrum makes early and frequent feeding sessions very important.

## SUCCESSFUL LATCHING-ON

Many components of a baby's sucking are a matter of reflex. (See page 16.) However, it is critical that the baby learn how to position herself, grip, and suck. Effective suckling doesn't always come automatically, and frequent exposure to an artificial nipple or pacifier might interfere with its

51

establishment. (See pages 57–59 for more information.)

## "LET-DOWN" REFLEX

Generally, milk doesn't flow from the breast the second the baby begins to suck. Often a few minutes will pass before the sucking triggers what is known as the let-down reflex. Stimulation on the baby's part and relaxation on the mother's cause the pituitary glands to release hormones. These hormones in turn cause the awaiting milk glands and ducts to let down the milk.

Many mothers experience this reflex as a not-unpleasant tingling, or pins-and-needles feeling around the tip of the breast, a feeling that fades as the nursing session progresses. The sensation frequently disappears altogether after a mother has been breastfeeding her child for a number of months. Whether you feel the tingling of the let-down, you'll know it's happening by listening to your baby's regular and satisfied gulps. If you have trouble getting let-down, some physicians recommend an artificial hormone in the form of a nose spray.

In the first few days or weeks of nursing, the same hormone that makes your milk flow will also cause your uterus to contract. It is normal to feel these "afterpains" when you nurse, and they will stop when your uterus has returned to a more normal postpartum state.

## SUPPLY AND DEMAND

The more your baby sucks and the more frequently she empties your breasts, the more milk you will make. Your milk production works on a supply-and-demand basis. It's especially important during the first weeks of your child's life to let her nurse as often as she desires so you can build up an adequate milk supply. Too frequent exposure to an artificial nipple when you're just establishing your milk supply can interfere with your baby's successful attachment to your breast. (See supplemental feedings, page 53.) If your baby is full of supplemental formula, she won't suck at your breasts, which will then be deprived of the signals they need to produce as much milk as your baby needs. If your baby seems hungry fairly soon after a nursing session, you should put her to the breast again. It won't be long before your breasts are producing enough milk to keep her full for a few hours. A few days after your milk comes in, your baby's frequent bowel movements will indicate a successful start to the breast-feeding.

## SCHEDULING

- Breast-fed babies should be nursed on demand—that is, according to their hunger. Signs of hunger include crying, moving the head toward the breast when held, and sucking.

- A newborn will need to nurse frequently—sometimes as many as a dozen or more times a day. Let her nurse often, because a mother's breasts need the frequent stimulation that the sucking gives to produce more milk.

- Some breast-fed babies fall into a fairly predictable feeding schedule after two or three weeks. A common pattern is nursing every two to four hours during the day, with a longer stretch of sleep at night. But not all babies readily establish a regular schedule, and those who do may still sometimes change schedules. Every baby is different; the right schedule is the one that keeps her happy.

- Even if your breast-fed baby has been nursing on a fairly regular schedule for a few weeks, it's normal for her to break that schedule suddenly and need to nurse more frequently. A growth spurt may signal her to suck more frequently. The new pattern will encourage your breasts to meet her increasing needs. Growth spurts typically take place at six weeks, three months, and six months of life.

## HOW LONG TO NURSE

Generally, an infant who is suckling effectively will get 90 percent of her milk in the first five to ten minutes of any given nursing session. But if it takes five minutes of sucking before your baby receives a significant amount of milk, you'll need to lengthen the time so that you're not ending a nursing session just as it actually gets started. Nutritive versus non-nutritive sucking, or a pacifying sucking, will be easier to distinguish as you become more proficient with feeds. Efficiency, not just time, is important in determining the number of minutes a baby should spend at feeding. You may need to seek help if your baby is not latching on correctly.

## WHICH BREAST FIRST?

Your baby will suck most vigorously at the first breast you offer her in a nursing session, because she's most hungry when she starts. Because this vigorous sucking is the best signal your breasts can receive to produce more milk, you'll want to make sure that both breasts are receiving equal signals. So alternate which breast you offer first at each nursing. A safety pin on the nursing bra to mark the side to begin on serves as a useful reminder to some mothers.

## VITAMIN SUPPLEMENTS

Some nursing mothers continue to take their prenatal vitamins to balance their diet, though this is not mandatory. Vitamin D, given directly to the baby, was commonly recommended in the past, but overall, breast milk is considered the optimal, nutritionally complete food. Many providers now say no vitamin or fluoride supplement is necessary.

## SUPPLEMENTAL FEEDINGS

During the first few weeks, you should devote yourself exclusively to getting your nursing baby onto the breast and sucking effectively. After a few weeks, however, an artificial nipple and bottle can be introduced. If you offer a bottle once or twice a week with either expressed breast milk or formula, it won't interfere with milk production, and it will allow your baby to feed well from either the breast or the bottle. As discussed in Chapter 2, pacifiers can be a comfort to babies. But over-frequent use in the first few days and weeks may confuse an infant. If your baby is slow to master nutritive suckling, be careful not to overuse a pacifier.

## EXPRESSING MILK

A variety of excellent breast pumps are available that express breast milk for later use. This process allows others besides the mother to feed the baby, which is especially helpful if the mother needs to return to work. Expressing milk, of course, also keeps your milk production up and can relieve breast fullness. The graduated cylinder-type pumps and the electric pumps (which are more feasible to rent than buy) are very effective, and you'll want to see which one is more suitable for you. Correct usage should not cause any pain or discomfort.

Milk that's been expressed can be stored in plastic nurser bags (with three to four ounces in each) in the freezer or refrigerator. Refrigerated milk should remain fresh for at least a day, and milk will keep in the freezer safely for several months, assuming the temperature remains sufficiently cold. Most babies prefer to drink milk warmed to at least room temperature. It's best to do this by placing the bag in warm water, not by using a microwave.

## CARE OF BREASTS

- You'll probably want to wear a nursing bra while you're breastfeeding your child for the convenience it offers. You'll especially want to make sure that any bra you wear while nursing fits well. A bra that presses or binds can clog milk ducts or even lead to a breast infection.

- Make sure your nipples are dry after each feeding. Leave them exposed to the air for fifteen minutes if possible.

- Carefully wash your breasts at least twice a day to remove any traces of milk. But don't use soap when you wash them; it removes natural oils and can lead to cracked nipples.

- If you're bothered by leaking nipples, you can keep your clothes dry by lining your bra with disposable cotton squares or breast pads. Don't use waterproof liners, and try to avoid bras that aren't cotton because they don't let air in.

## ENGORGEMENT

When the milk first comes in (usually in two to six days), your breasts will frequently feel exceptionally full. Even though this feeling subsides within a few days, it can be an uncomfortable, painful experience. By all means, let your baby nurse as much as she wants to. This is the best way to empty your breasts and increase your comfort. Additionally, you

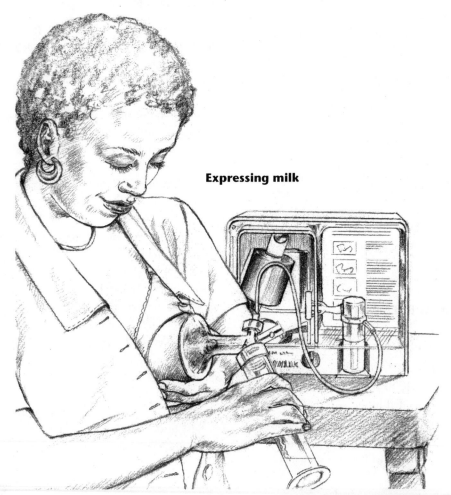

**Expressing milk**

may need to express some milk manually either before or during a feeding. Some women also find a warm shower or warm washcloths on the breasts help milk flow. In severe cases, however, these methods can increase blood flow and pain, in which case application of cool compresses may be more pleasant. After the first few days, you may also feel engorged when your baby goes too long between feedings. The same treatments will work then.

## SORE NIPPLES

Sore nipples are common among breast-feeding mothers, even those with their second or third child. The soreness can last several days. To prevent soreness, make sure your baby masters the technique of positioning the nipple appropriately in the mouth. (See page 57.) If a cracked or particularly sore area develops, try changing the baby's positions while nursing. This will move the tension to slightly different areas. Also, wash your nipples with water only and let them dry by exposing them to air after washing or nursing. You may need to limit the nursing sessions to five to ten minutes at a time.

## MASTITIS

Mastitis is a bacterial infection of the breast that can occur as a result of a clogged milk duct. The breast will become red and tender, and the infection can cause fever, aches, and nausea. The recommended treatment is to continue nursing your baby, as removing the milk will help resolve the infection. If nursing is extremely painful, nurse on the opposite, unaffected side alone. You should also contact your physician, who will prescribe antibiotics to clear up the infection. Mastitis will not have any adverse effect on your baby.

## BITING

Once a breast-fed baby gets upper and lower teeth, she may start biting your nipples while she's nursing. It's important to remember that this is in no way malicious, nor does it suggest that your child wants to be weaned. Her new teeth, or teeth that have yet to break through, may be bothering her gums, and she simply feels better biting on anything she can get her mouth around.

No one is going to pretend that biting doesn't hurt or that it should be ignored. It typically happens, though, at the end of a nursing session when a child has had enough to eat and is simply playing around. So gently, but firmly, say "no" to your child as soon as you feel any biting and remove her from the breast. Using this approach consistently will teach most babies not to bite.

## SUPPORT FOR MOTHER

Although breastfeeding your baby is the most natural thing in the world, it still requires commitment and work. Some women become discouraged by engorgement or infection. Working mothers may feel expressing milk is too time consuming. Some feel tied down to their babies, as though they can't go anywhere because they must be there for the next feeding.

Breastfeeding mothers need emotional support, as well as information. La Leche League is a national organization designed to provide you with that support and encouragement. Most communities have a local chapter that holds meetings on a regular basis. More and more, health care facilities and communities also have certified lactation specialists who can help establish and support proper breastfeeding. Clinics often have identified support staff as well.

# What a Nursing Mother Needs

## REST

Adequate rest is essential to a good milk supply, especially during those early postpartum weeks, when you're still recovering. Get some extra sleep when your baby naps, and try to ignore all of those things you'd like to get done.

## RELAXATION

Work at being relaxed and unruffled, especially just before you nurse your baby. Emotional tensions can interfere with your let-down reflex and can keep your baby from getting the milk she needs. A comfortable chair and some soothing music may help in this regard.

## LIQUIDS

Nursing mothers need to drink plenty of liquids (six to eight glasses a day). It's a good idea to get into the habit of drinking a glass of water or unsweetened fruit juice before or with each nursing session. You will probably notice that you feel thirsty more often than usual while you are nursing. Pale yellow urine is a good indicator you are drinking enough.

## DIET

Your breast milk can contain only the vitamins and minerals you provide for it, and your body needs help to recover from childbirth. A nursing mother needs about 2,500 calories a day—200 to 500 more than the number needed during pregnancy. This diet should include about sixty-five grams of protein and plenty of calcium. A guideline for your diet follows.*

| FOOD GROUPS | DAILY SERVINGS | SOURCES |
|---|---|---|
| Dairy | 4 to 5 servings | Cheese, custard, milk, pudding, yogurt |
| Protein sources | 2 to 3 servings | Fish, dried beans, lean beef or pork, lentils, nuts, peanut butter, poultry, eggs |
| Fruits and vegetables | 7 to 8 servings with 1 high in vitamin C | Avocado, corn, green leafy vegetables, beans, melons, oranges, peas, strawberries, kiwi, potatoes |
| Grains | 6 to 11 servings | Bread, bulgar, cereals, pancakes, pasta, rice |
| Sweets and fats | Moderate amounts | Chips, cookies, candy |

*Teen mothers who nurse will need more dairy and protein. Mothers of twins need to add 1,000 calories to this daily diet.

* Some foods in your diet could cause problems for your child:
  * You may want to limit so-called gassy foods, such as cabbage, broccoli, garlic, and onions.
  * Caffeine can cause temporary fussiness in babies.
  * Some infants may show an allergy to cows' milk protein in their mothers' diet. If you think your baby is allergic, take cows' milk out of your diet for a while to see if allergy symptoms go away.
  * Nursing mothers should abstain completely from alcohol and nicotine. If you do drink, moderation is a must.

# Nursing Positions—Cradle Hold Step-by-Step

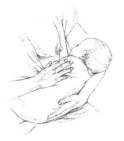

**1** SIT DOWN with your baby in a comfortable chair. Place the side of your baby's head in the crook of your arm. Bring the hand of that arm around him. You and your baby should be abdomen to abdomen. Wrap his bottom arm around your side, so it does not get between the two of you.

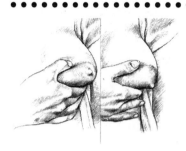

**2** SUPPORT your breast with your free hand by placing the fingers under your breast and your thumb on top. Keep them all behind the areola by at least two inches. Another method is to do a "scissors" hold, using two fingers—one above and one below—to make the areola and nipple protrude.

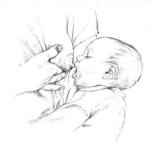

**3** PULL your baby close to you. Tickle your baby's upper lip very lightly with your nipple until the mouth is open wide.

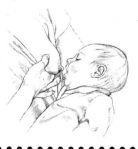

**4** CENTER your nipple and your baby will latch onto it. When centering your nipple, you will be able to alter its position by pressing your thumb in to move it up or pressing your fingers in to move it down.

**5** WHEN your baby's mouth is on the breast properly, the bottom lip will curl out.

# Nursing Positions—Lying Down Step-by-Step

**1**    LIE DOWN on your side on a bed or roomy couch with pillows around your head and shoulders.

**2**    CURVE your body slightly so your baby can fit comfortably next to you.

**3**    LAY the baby on her side, slightly raising and supporting her head in the crook of your arm. Wrap your forearm around her and draw her feet close to you so that she's angled into the curve of your body. This will help keep her nose free to breathe while she's nursing.

**4**    BE SURE you're relaxed, supported entirely by the bed and pillows, not by your own back muscles or elbow. Then follow cradle-hold instructions 4 and 5 for centering your baby on the nipple.

# Nursing Positions—Football Hold Step-by-Step

**1** BE SURE to use a comfortable, well-padded easy chair or rocker. You may want to put a pillow behind your back for support or under your baby to bring her into a more convenient nursing position.

**2** AVOID bending over while nursing. It will make you tense, and you'll end up with a backache.

**3** SUPPORT your baby in the football position (see page 20), turning your baby toward you at your side. Mothers recovering from a Cesarean delivery often prefer this method because it keeps the baby off the abdomen.

**4** MAKE SURE that her head is well-supported and that she's sitting at a slight angle, with her head higher than her stomach. This makes air bubbles burp up more easily. Then follow the cradle-hold instruction 4 and 5 for centering your baby on the nipple.

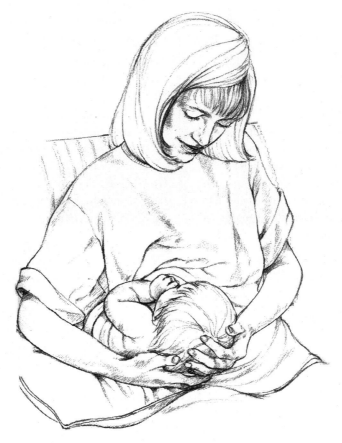

# Weaning from the Breast

## WHEN?

There is no uniform time for weaning all babies. The right time may vary from a few weeks to a few years in actual practice. Only you can decide what will work best for you and your child. Many babies will wean themselves when they're ready. This is often the least traumatic and most conflict-free way to wean, if you have the leisure. If the weaning is more your choice, your baby may need additional attention, especially if you have been nursing for a long time. Try to give your child all the extra cuddling and care you can.

## HOW?

How you wean is more important than when you wean. Be sure to do it gradually, gently, and with plenty of love and patience.

- Be as flexible as you can with the weaning. If at all possible, don't establish strict goals or rigid schedules.

- You'll want to avoid sudden weaning for two reasons. It can cause a dramatic decline in the mother's hormonal flow, and it may trigger depression, which is compounded by the abrupt loss of the special, close nursing relationship. Sudden weaning can also be traumatic for the child who has learned to gain comfort and solace, as well as nourishment, from the breast.

- When you wean, gradually cut back one feeding at a time. The lunch-time feeding is usually the first to go. Offer your baby milk or juice from a cup or a bottle in addition to food (if your baby has started on solids). Every two to three days, substitute another bottle or cup feeding for the breastfeeding.

Many babies can be weaned entirely in one to two weeks.

- If you're weaning from the breast to formula or cows' milk, and your baby doesn't seem to like the taste, try a mixture of half breast milk and half formula or cows' milk.

- Many babies cling the longest to the nighttime or first morning feeding.

- A baby weaned early may miss sucking, especially at bedtime, in which case you may want to offer a cup, bottle, or pacifier, though the bottle should never be given to the baby in bed.

- Breast-fed babies, unless they're very young, often don't need to transfer from breast to bottle. They can be weaned directly to a cup. A weighted, two-handled cup with a spout is ideal for the inexperienced drinker.

- If you're weaning your baby gradually, you shouldn't suffer the discomfort of engorged breasts. (See page 54.) But if you do happen to become uncomfortable because of a missed feeding, express some milk from your breasts—just until you're fairly comfortable again. (See page 55.) Don't express too much, or you'll stimulate even more milk production.

- If your baby is progressing well with weaning and suddenly suffers from teething or a cold, don't be surprised at your baby's renewed need to nurse. You'll certainly not want to deny her this comfort while she's miserable; when she starts to feel better, the weaning can resume where you left off.

# Bottlefeeding Basics

You can feed a baby either formula or expressed breast milk from a bottle. An earlier section on breastfeeding discussed expressing milk for later use. Although this section will concentrate on bottlefeeding with infant formula, you can also follow the procedures on pages 66–67 if you're giving expressed breast milk to your baby.

## KINDS OF FORMULA

Infant formulas contain the major nutrients that babies need. Because vitamins are added to formulas, no vitamin supplement is necessary. If either powdered or liquid concentrate forms are used, your baby will get all the fluoride she needs from the water supply. (If your water is not fluoridated, a supplement may be prescribed.)

Commercially prepared formulas fall into three main categories:

- The first category consists of cows' milk-based formulas made with cows' milk protein and lactose sugar. The design of these formulas makes them more digestible and less allergenic.

- The second category consists of formulas made with soy protein and non-lactose sugar. These formulas are recommended in some instances for babies allergic to cows' milk or recovering from diarrhea.

- A third category consists of formulas for babies with special needs.

Cows' milk formulas come with different amounts of iron. The American Academy of Pediatrics recommends that you use iron-fortified formulas, not low-iron formulas, for the first year. You may worry that your baby will become constipated on formula with iron, because some mothers become constipated while taking iron during their pregnancy. Actually, iron can cause either diarrhea or constipation but usually causes neither. Continue giving your baby iron-fortified formula despite stool consistency; if constipation becomes a problem, you can handle it in other ways. (See page 103.)

Infant formulas are available in three forms:

- Powdered formulas can be mixed with tap water, are light to carry and easy to store, are the least expensive of formulas, and are available in 12-ounce, 14-ounce, or 16-ounce (340-gm, 400-gm, or 454-gm) cans, and single-feeding packets.

- Liquid concentrates can be mixed with tap water, are easy to prepare, and are available in 13-fluid-ounce (384-ml) cans.

- Ready-to-use formulas can be poured directly into bottles and used without any mixing. More expensive than powdered or liquid concentrate formulas, they are available in 8- or 32-fluid-ounce (256- to 946-ml) cans and 4- and 8-fluid-ounce (128- or 256-ml) bottles.

## STORING FORMULA

- Once you've opened a container of *liquid* or *ready-to-use* formula and prepared a batch of bottles, you should cover and store the remaining formula in the refrigerator. You should throw away any refrigerated formula after it has been open forty-eight hours.

- Once you've opened a can of *powdered* formula, you should cover the can and store it in a cool, dry place. The can will indicate how long you can use the formula.

- After you've prepared a bottle of formula, either use it immediately or refrigerate it. You can safely use refrigerated bottled formula for twenty-four to forty-eight hours after preparation.

- You can leave a bottle at room temperature for up to an hour without worrying about bacterial build-up in the formula (a half-hour in hot weather). If your baby has taken part of it, be sure to throw it away after an hour. But if she hasn't touched it, you can safely put it back in the refrigerator and use it later.

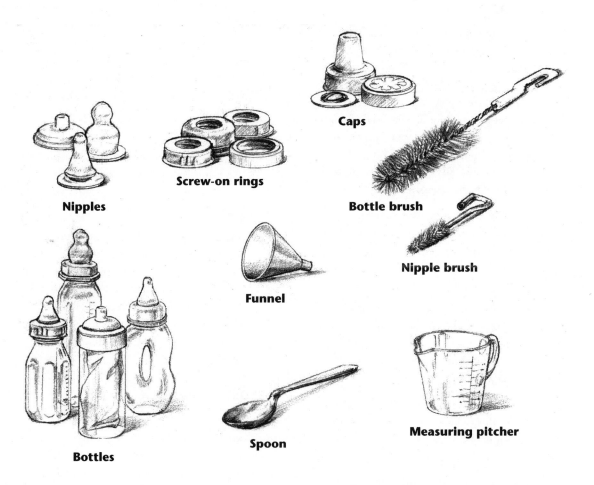

Nipples

Screw-on rings

Caps

Bottle brush

Nipple brush

Funnel

Bottles

Spoon

Measuring pitcher

# Preparing Formula

- As long as you clean the feeding equipment you use regularly and are careful to wash your hands in hot, soapy water before you prepare a batch of formula, there's no need to sterilize any of the equipment or the water you use. Common sense and good personal hygiene are sufficient.

- Be sure to mix the formula exactly as your physician prescribes or as the formula manufacturer recommends. Formula that is too concentrated or too dilute can cause health problems for the baby.

- Prepare powdered or liquid concentrates using the procedures described below. Ready-to-use formulas need no preparation; you simply pour them into clean bottles.

The equipment needed to bottle-feed your baby depends in part on what kind of formula you use. The basic equipment required is listed below (see also previous page):

- Eight to ten 8-ounce (240-ml) bottles. Both glass and plastic bottles are available. You can also use disposable bottles, which are plastic, sterilized sacks that you can buy in a roll, tear off, use once in a special holder, and then throw away.

- Eight to ten caps or covers

- Eight to ten screw-on rings

- Eight to ten nipples

- A bottle brush

- A nipple brush

- A measuring pitcher that is graduated in ounces (or ml), preferably one with a cover

- A funnel

- A large, long-handled spoon

## CARE FOR EQUIPMENT

- Thoroughly rinse the formula from each bottle immediately after it's used.

- Using the bottle and nipple brushes and hot, soapy water, wash each bottle, ring, and nipple separately. Carefully squeeze water through the nipples to make sure you remove all milk residue. Or, wash everything in the dishwasher.

- Rinse everything in hot, clean water and let air dry.

# Preparing Formula
# Step-by-Step

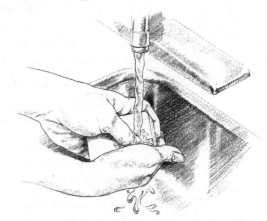

**1** WASH your hands thoroughly with soap and hot water. If you're opening a can of concentrated formula, clean the top of the can.

**2** FOLLOW directions on the cans or bottles of formula. This will usually mean preparing a whole batch of bottles at once. Pour the formula into clean bottles if you're preparing a whole batch. A funnel makes the job easier.

**3** PUT the nipples (inverted), caps, and rings on the bottles. Store the bottles in the refrigerator. (See section on storing formula, page 61.)

# How to Bottle-Feed

## HOW MUCH?

- Try to stay a bit ahead of your baby in how much formula you offer. Begin by offering three ounces (90 ml) at each feeding, and as soon as she starts emptying the bottle at two or three feedings each day, start adding half an ounce (15 ml) of formula to each bottle. With time, she will work herself up to eight ounces (240 ml) a feeding. Generally, you can follow the rough guidelines below for the first year. But remember to let her decide how much she wants.

- Don't worry if your baby doesn't take much formula at any given feeding. Just as your appetite fluctuates, so does your baby's. If, on occasion, she's happy and thriving in every other way but doesn't touch a bottle, it's nothing to worry about.

- Sometimes a baby will stop sucking in the middle of a feeding. Don't mistake this for lack of interest. She's probably just resting. Be patient, and when she's ready, she'll start eating again. But don't force a bottle if it's clear she doesn't want any more, and don't nudge every last drop of formula into your infant if it's clear she's not interested.

## SCHEDULING AND DEMAND

- Bottle-fed babies will usually go from two to four hours between feedings, and will eventually go for a longer stretch at night.

- Imposing a strict feeding schedule on a young bottle-fed baby is not a good idea, because it may result in more anxiety for the mother or father and more discomfort for the newborn than are necessary. Offering a bottle to a baby whenever she seems hungry will not spoil her. Just make sure her needs do not lie elsewhere, such as needing a change of diaper, a warmer room, or simply some cuddling. Her digestive system will soon adjust to a two- to four-hour schedule that you can count on, and that will lengthen as she gets older.

- Don't wake your baby in the middle of the night for a feeding. If she's hungry, she'll wake herself.

| AGE | AMOUNT PER DAY |
| --- | --- |
| Birth to 1 month | 18–24 oz. (540-720 ml) |
| 1 to 2 months | 22–26 oz. (660-780 ml) |
| 2 to 3 months | 24–26 oz. (720-780 ml) |
| 3 to 4 months | 24–28 oz. (720-840 ml) |
| 4 to 5 months | 24–30 oz. (720-900 ml) |
| 5 to 6 months | 24–32 oz. (720-960 ml) |
| 6 months to 1 year | 24–32 oz. (720-960 ml) |

# Giving the Bottle to Your Baby

- Although you can give formula to your baby at almost any temperature, she may prefer it slightly warm. If you're making up a bottle of formula using tap water, simply draw water at the desired temperature. If you want to warm up a cold bottle, just set it in a pan of water on the stove for a few minutes or set the bottle in a pan in the sink and run hot water over it. Warming bottles in a microwave is not a good idea because heating can be uneven, and bottles may break. Test the formula on the inside of your wrist to make sure it's not too hot. Hot milk, of course, can scald a baby's tongue and mouth.

- Check the flow of milk from the nipple at each feeding. The milk should drip out steadily—initially about one drop per second. If it comes out too slowly, your baby will tire of sucking before she's had her fill and will probably swallow a lot of air in the process. You can enlarge a nipple hole with a hot needle. If the milk comes out too quickly, your baby will be full before she sucks as much as she needs to. And she may try to slow the stream of milk by thrusting her tongue up against the nipple. Doing this can affect the placement of her teeth and harm later tooth development. Throw away the nipple if the milk flows too quickly.

- It's important that air get into the bottle and displace the formula. Otherwise, the baby will not be able to suck anything out. So keep the bottle cap slightly loose to allow air to enter. You can tell that your baby is successfully feeding if you observe a constant stream of bubbles rising through the formula, whether it be in a disposable bag or traditional bottle.

- Avoid propping a bottle or teaching your young infant to hold it herself. If left alone with a bottle, an infant could choke on the formula. And, more importantly, every baby vitally needs cuddling and love to accompany a feeding.

- Avoid putting your baby to bed with a bottle. A baby who feeds lying down has a greater tendency to get an ear infection. And falling asleep with a bottle in her mouth can lead to tooth decay, even if your baby's teeth have not yet erupted.

# Step-by-Step

**1** TO INTRODUCE a bottle to your baby, hold her in your lap, circled in the crook of your arm, and gently touch the cheek nearest you with the nipple of the bottle. This will trigger her rooting reflex (see page 16), and she'll turn toward you with an open mouth, searching for the nipple.

**2** BE SURE to hold your baby with her head and upper body raised at a slight angle while you feed her. It's easier for her to swallow the milk in this position than if she's lying flat on her back.

**3** TRY to keep the neck of the bottle constantly filled with milk by tipping it upward as you feed your baby. This helps keep her from swallowing too much air. When it's clear that your baby is finished, proceed to burp her. (See page 68.)

# Burping and Spitting Up

- When a baby takes a bottle or nurses, she often swallows air that can make her uncomfortable until she burps it up.

- Unless your baby is unusually fussy, one burp during a feeding and one burp after are usually enough. Bottle-fed babies can be burped after every 2–3 ounces.

- Try not to interrupt your baby's feeding to burp her. Take advantage of her pauses in sucking and use them as burp times. If you're breastfeeding, try to burp her before you switch her to your other breast.

- It is not always necessary to get a burp from your baby. If one does not come up in a few minutes, resume feeding her and try again later if she's fussy.

- Before you burp your baby, drape a diaper or towel across your shoulder or knees to catch anything she may spit up.

- When you put your baby down after a feeding, be sure to place her on her stomach or side. This allows any trapped air to escape more easily, and prevents choking on any milk or mucus she does spit up. Be careful, however, about leaving your baby on her stomach if she is going to sleep. (See sleep positions, pages 37–38.)

- Handle your baby gently after a feeding. Bouncing or jiggling her may cause her to spit up milk with a burp.

- Spitting up some milk with a burp is quite common among infants. When it's not the result of too much swallowed air or too large a meal, it is often due to the relaxation of the muscles that control the passage between the stomach and the esophagus—known medically as reflux. In any case, your baby will spit up less and less as she grows, so if she's thriving and content in every other way, it's nothing to worry about. Spitting up, in contrast to vomiting, refers to a nonforceful flow of stomach contents. On the other hand, vomiting is associated with vigorous muscle contraction and loss of most of the volume of a feeding.

- If your baby seems to be spitting up unusually large amounts of milk, try holding her in a more upright position when you feed her, so that the air she swallows is not trapped below the milk in her stomach. It also helps to keep your baby at a more upright angle—while she is still leaning forward or to the side—for at least a half hour after feeding, if spitting up is a problem.

- If a bottle-fed baby is spitting up, you may be overfeeding her.

# Burping Methods

**OPTION 1** HOLD your baby with her head over your shoulder. Gently rub or pat her back until she burps.

**OPTION 2** SET your baby upright but leaning slightly forward on your lap. Be sure to support her head and back. Gently rub or pat her back until she burps.

**OPTION 3** LAY your baby face-down across your lap or a mattress. Turn her head to one side and support it with one hand. Gently rub or pat her back until she burps.

# Weaning from the Bottle

## WHEN?

There is no absolute right age to wean a baby from the bottle, but it can be comfortably done as soon as the baby is old enough to drink milk from a cup. Using a cup is a good way to improve hand-to-mouth coordination. Furthermore, weaning earlier rather than later can prevent the bottle from becoming a "security" object. Many bottle-fed babies can be introduced to a cup as early as five or six months of age and be off the bottle entirely by one year.

Gazing around while sucking on the bottle, mouthing instead of sucking the nipple, and trying to move away before a bottle is done may be signs the baby is ready to wean.

## HOW?

How you wean your baby is just as important as when you do it. Be sure to do it gradually and gently, with plenty of love and patience.

- Weaning from the bottle is often easily done by occasionally introducing liquids, formula, breast milk, or water out of a cup. A weighted, two-handled cup with a spout is ideal for the inexperienced drinker. A small plastic cup also works well for some infants.

- If your infant is strongly attached to the bottle and refuses to take milk from a cup, don't despair. Just continue offering it to her. Though it may seem like a toy at first, you can help demonstrate its use as a means to drink. Keep your attitude casual, and when she does start taking a sip or two, which she eventually will, don't force more. She'll catch on at her own pace.

- Weaning will be easier if, once your baby is mobile, you let her have a bottle only while you're holding her in your lap. You'll need to be firm, but her delight in her new-found motor skills will gradually supersede her interest in the bottle.

- When you wean gradually, cut back one feeding at a time. Offer your baby her milk or juice from a cup, along with the solid foods you give her at mealtime. It may help to reduce the amount you normally put in the bottle before you change to the cup.

- The lunch-time feeding is usually the first to go. Many babies cling the longest to the bedtime feeding, others to the first morning bottle.

- If you're progressing along well with weaning, and your child suddenly suffers from teething or a cold, don't be surprised if she shows an increased need for the bottle. You'll certainly not want to deny that source of comfort while she's miserable. When she starts feeling better, she'll soon be able to pick up weaning where she left off.

# Introducing Solid Food

## WHEN?

Babies are usually ready for solid foods when they're four to six months old. By then the digestive system is developed enough to handle solids, and infants begin to need the additional calories and nutrients that solid foods offer. Your baby will often give cues when she's ready for solids. Breast milk or formula won't completely satisfy her, or she'll want more nursing sessions or formula feedings, an interest that won't subside in two or three days (as it will with a growth spurt). New teeth make a baby eager to chew and suggest a readiness for more than breast milk or formula.

## WHY WAIT?

It is important not to introduce solids too soon for a number of reasons:

- For young babies, breast milk is the ideal, and formula the most nearly ideal food they can have. Feeding an infant solids too soon only fills her up with inferior foods, and she could suffer nutritionally.

- Delaying the introduction of solid foods helps avoid food-induced allergies and allergic manifestations, such as eczema and asthma.

- It is possible that introducing solid foods too early may contribute to obesity later on.

- Despite rumor, it has never been clearly demonstrated that giving cereal at bedtime during infancy will help a baby sleep through the night.

## HOW TO INTRODUCE SOLIDS

- Introduce solid foods while your baby is still getting a substantial amount of nourishment from breast milk or formula. That way, you can feel comfortable experimenting with solids. At first

**FOOD GUIDE PYRAMID**

Suggested Daily Servings

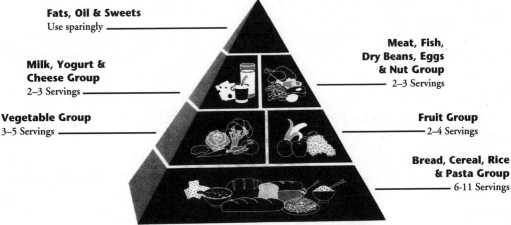

Fats, Oil & Sweets
Use sparingly

Meat, Fish, Dry Beans, Eggs & Nut Group
2–3 Servings

Milk, Yogurt & Cheese Group
2–3 Servings

Vegetable Group
3–5 Servings

Fruit Group
2–4 Servings

Bread, Cereal, Rice & Pasta Group
6-11 Servings

Source: U.S. Department of Agriculture/U.S. Department of Health and Human Services

you'll want to offer solids in addition to, not in the place of, breast milk or formula.

- Don't force solid foods on your baby. She'll eat when her body needs them. In fact, the whole goal of introducing solid foods should be to make mealtime an enjoyable, stress-free activity.

- Respect your baby as an individual. Even at six months, she'll display preferences and enjoy variety.

- At first, be sure to introduce solid foods one at a time, and then wait a few days after each new food to make sure it doesn't cause an allergic reaction. Avoid stews, soups, or multigrain cereals when you're starting out; if your baby has an allergic reaction to one of these, you won't know exactly which food caused it.

## FOOD INTOLERANCE AND ALLERGIC REACTIONS

If your baby begins wheezing or develops rashes, a sore bottom, or diarrhea, and you've just introduced a new food in the last day or two, you may be seeing an allergic reaction. Most food reactions are mild and no cause for alarm. Just make sure you don't give your child that food for several more months, and then reintroduce it at first in very small amounts. However, if your child's reaction is severe, or you're in doubt, be sure to contact your health care provider.

## COMMON SOURCES OF FOOD ALLERGIES

The most common sources of food allergies in infants are cows' milk and egg whites. In addition, wheat, corn, pork, fish, shellfish, onions, citrus fruits, nuts, and strawberries can also cause allergic reactions in babies. In general, you may want to delay offering any of these foods to your child before age one. If you have a family history of allergies to any of these foods, you'll want to consult your physician before you offer it to your child.

## OTHER FOODS TO AVOID

For other reasons, you should also avoid introducing the following foods to an infant:

- Honey, which is possibly connected to the occurrence of a disease called infant botulism. Do not offer it during your baby's first year.

- Nuts and popcorn or any other food that could cause your infant to choke.

- Heavily sweetened foods, such as soda, lemonade, or baby food desserts.

## FEEDING SCHEDULES

- Start offering your baby solid foods once a day. Midmorning or midafternoon is ideal. That way, you won't be distracted by the rush of family mealtimes. Don't offer foods right after bottlefeeding or nursing; your baby will be satisfied already and less likely to be interested.

- After a couple of weeks, increase the frequency to twice a day.

- After about a month of trying solids, start offering them in between a nursing or bottlefeeding session. Your baby will have a better appetite for them then, while still not being ravenously hungry.

- At this point, observe your child's appetite and degree of satisfaction with what you're offering. If you patiently allow her to set the pace, she'll gradually wean herself from all-milk meals to regular meals with the family.

| AGE | AMOUNTS OF FOOD PER DAY |
| --- | --- |
| **6 to 7 months** | Breast milk or iron-fortified formula |
| | Baby rice cereal mixed with breast milk or formula (up to 8 tbsp.) |
| | Noncitrus juice (2–4 oz.) |
| | Strained fruits and cooked vegetables (up to 8 tbsp.) |
| **8 to 9 months** | Breast milk or iron-fortified formula |
| | Baby cereal mixed with breast milk or formula (8 tbsp.) |
| | Juices, including citrus juices (2–4 oz.) |
| | Strained to finely chopped fruits and cooked vegetables; bite-size pieces when ready (6–8 tbsp.) |
| | Strained meats and puréed egg yolks (4 tbsp.—no whites until one year old) |
| **10 months to 1 year** | Breast milk or iron-fortified formula |
| | Baby cereal mixed with breast milk or formula (6–8 tbsp.) |
| | Juice (2–4 oz.) |
| | Mashed or bite-size fruits and cooked vegetables (6–8 tbsp.) |
| | Ground or chopped meat and meat substitutes, such as egg yolks (1–2 oz.) |
| | Potato and whole-grain or enriched-grain products |

## HOW MUCH FOOD?

- Introduce solids to your child in small amounts, such as one to two teaspoons (5 to 10 ml), until she gets used to the taste and the practice. Make the consistency of the food rather watery by diluting it with breast milk or formula.

- Increase the amount gradually to four to six tablespoons (60 to 90 ml) as she becomes more accomplished at eating and as her appetite for solids increases. (A small jar of commercial baby food typically contains eight tablespoons—128 ml—of food.) Use the chart on the previous page as a rough guideline for the first year of life.

- Never force your child to eat nor try to slip in one last bite when it's clear she's had enough.

- You'll be able to tell when your child is finished with her meal by her behavior. She'll turn her head away from the spoon or close her lips tightly and refuse to take anything more into her mouth. Crying, gagging, or spitting the food out may suggest your baby doesn't want more food, but these signs may also indicate that she hasn't quite learned how to eat solids yet, or that your feeding technique needs improvement.

## HOW TO SPOON-FEED

A breast-fed or bottle-fed baby knows of feeding entirely in terms of sucking, so give her some time to catch on to using a spoon. The best way to introduce spoon-feeding is to place a small dab of food on the tip of a small baby spoon or demitasse spoon. Place the spoon just between the baby's lips and then let her suck the food off. She'll soon become experienced enough to receive the food from the spoon directly into her mouth.

## A NOTE ABOUT MESSES

Babies are messy eaters. The more you try to fight that, the more unhappy mealtimes will become for both you and your child. So be prepared and you'll be freed from much of the dismay. You may want to line the floor around your child's eating area with newspapers. A bib on your baby and an apron on yourself helps. Most important, though, is a relaxed attitude and an eye for making mealtimes enjoyable, whatever the mess.

## WHAT KINDS OF FOODS?

A little rice cereal mixed with breast milk or formula is the most common first food to introduce to a baby. Iron-fortified cereals are good for meeting your baby's iron needs. (Don't put foods, such as cereal, into bottles, unless your physician has specifically advised you to do so. This teaches babies to drink solids, which is not a good practice.)

Once your child becomes comfortable eating rice cereal, you can expand the menu in a number of directions. Here are some common possibilities:

- Various cereals, such as barley, millet, or oatmeal, moistened with breast milk or formula.

- Mashed white potatoes, mixed with breast milk or formula.

- Sweet potatoes or winter squash, mashed and moistened with apple juice or water.

- Other vegetables, such as cooked carrots, skinned beets, peas, and spinach, all mashed or puréed.

- Fruits, such as apples, peaches, and pears, that are peeled and then cooked into a sauce or puréed.

- Puréed, mashed, or finely chopped meats, moistened with a little water or juice from the meat.

- Egg yolk, cooked and mashed with a little water, breast milk, or formula. Be sure to avoid offering egg whites until your baby is at least one year old. Egg whites are one of the most common sources of allergies when introduced too early.

Once your baby has comfortably gone this far and is happily eating, you can offer her many of the foods that the family is eating. Experiment carefully, however, with gas-producing foods like broccoli, cabbage, and onions.

## VITAMIN SUPPLEMENTS

The best way to get necessary vitamins is through a balanced diet. Once your baby starts eating a variety of solid foods, you can stop administering any vitamin supplements you may be administering, unless your health care provider instructs otherwise. Do make sure your baby has some source of fluoride after six months of age.

## PREPARING BABY FOODS AT HOME

No one will disagree that home-prepared baby foods are cheaper and fresher than commercially prepared foods. With a baby-food grinder or a food processor, you can quickly turn almost any of the foods you eat into something your baby will enjoy.

## COMMERCIAL FOODS

Commercially prepared baby foods are convenient and sterilized, and they frequently contain vitamin and mineral supplements. Although most manufacturers have removed unnecessary additives, you'll still want to check the labels to make sure there's no added salt, sugar, or other preservatives.

It's generally recommended that you use a jar of baby food within one to two days of opening it. Don't feed your baby directly from a jar you plan to use again, because the saliva from your baby's mouth will hasten the growth of bacteria in the food.

## WARMING BABY FOODS

It's not necessary to heat foods; in fact, your baby may prefer them at room temperature. If you do want to warm the food, however, you can set a jar of it in a pan of water on the stove or heat it in a microwave, but be very careful not to overheat it. You can also buy a plastic feeding dish that you fill with warm water to keep food hot.

## FINGER FOOD

With the advent of a few teeth and the necessary hand coordination, your baby will want to try feeding herself. This usually happens at around eight to twelve months, although often she'll be able to handle crackers or hard, dry toast a little earlier. Below is a list of finger foods that are nutritious, easy to handle when offered in small bites, and appropriate for stomachs just getting used to solid foods.

- Chopped chicken livers
- Shreds of chicken pieces
- Boned fish
- Egg yolks
- Peanut butter on whole wheat toast
- Hamburger
- Diced beef, veal, and lamb
- Bananas
- Cooked pieces of apples, pears, and peaches
- Ripe avocado
- Mashed potatoes
- Macaroni
- Lima beans
- Tofu (soybean curd)
- Sugarless, dried cereal

# Preparing Baby Foods

**TIPS**

- To prevent bacterial contamination, prepare the foods on a very clean surface. Avoid wooden cutting boards that have been used for preparing meat.
- Don't add sugar, salt, or other seasonings to the baby food you make.
- Be sure to freeze foods that will not be used within 24 hours. Ice cube trays come in handy for freezing individual portions.

# Step-by-Step

**1** COOK the meats, fruits, or vegetables you plan to offer your child. You can use canned fruits and vegetables, but they're not as nutritious as fresh or frozen foods.

**2** PURÉE, grind, mash, or finely chop the cooked foods in a blender, food processor, or baby-food grinder. Make sure that the texture of the food is right for your beginning eater. Food that's too coarse can cause choking. The more experienced your child gets at eating, the coarser the texture you can offer.

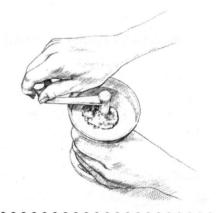

**3** SPOON the puréed food into an ice cube tray and freeze it. When the cubes are frozen, you can store them in plastic bags in the freezer and use them one at a time. (Just reheat them in a pan or in the microwave.)

# CHAPTER 4

# Your Baby's Safety

Because of improved preventive health care and other advances in medicine, diseases that formerly killed infants have been largely eliminated or controlled. Today, accidents kill more children than the next five causes of death combined, and automobile accidents are by far the leading cause of death and injury to children under the age of four.

Your objective should be to provide a safe environment that your child can explore. As a parent, the most important thing you can do is make sure you put your baby into an approved car seat when you travel. It's also important that you anticipate your child's development, so you can childproof your house before he enters a new stage. On the pages that follow, you'll find a complete guide to child-proofing your home, plus information on buying safety-oriented baby equipment.

Newborn babies are totally helpless and need to be protected at all times. As a baby begins to wiggle, roll over, grasp objects, creep, and eventually crawl, accidents tend to happen more often. Children are naturally curious and active, but their balance and sense of danger don't develop until they're older. They need to be able to explore their environment in a safe and carefully supervised way.

Below is a general outline of a baby's typical development during the first year. Details are provided in Chapter 5.

| | |
|---|---|
| **Birth through 2 months** | Your baby will wiggle and may start to roll over. |
| **3 through 5 months** | Your baby will begin to rock and roll over, grasp things, and put things into his mouth. |
| **6 through 9 months** | Your baby will begin to creep, crawl, pull himself up, and pull everything else down. |
| **10 through 12 months** | Your baby will begin to stand, climb, and possibly even walk. |

# Childproofing Your Home

## GENERAL SAFETY TIPS

Here is a thorough list of general child-proofing guidelines for your home, followed by specific tips covering the different areas of a home.

- Cover unused outlets with safety caps. Use safety covers over outlets with electric plugs in them.

- Put bulbs in all empty light sockets.

- Don't let your baby near electrical appliances when they are in use. Always turn off such appliances when they are no longer being used.

- Keep pins, buttons, screws, beads, coins, marbles, and other small or sharp objects out of your baby's reach. It only takes a minute for a crawling or creeping baby to put a button in his mouth and choke. Also, never feed your infant nuts or popcorn.

- Keep scissors, knives, razor blades, tools, and all breakable or broken objects out of your baby's reach.

- Keep all plastic bags and sheets of thin plastic out of your baby's reach. Never cover the crib mattress with thin plastic. Throw out or lock up plastic bags from the dry cleaners.

- Never leave a baby unattended with a balloon. Once a balloon has popped, remove all pieces immediately, so your baby doesn't choke on them.

- Appliance cords, telephone cords, cords from blinds, and other cords or straps can strangle babies. Keep them out of your baby's reach. Watch him carefully when he's playing with a toy that has a cord.

- Never put necklaces, cords attached to pacifiers, or cords of any kind around your baby's neck.

- Make sure there are no used ashtrays, glasses containing wine or other liquor, matches, or cigarette lighters in rooms where your baby is playing.

- Don't smoke while caring for your baby. Cigarettes can burn your child, and the smoke from them can irritate an infant's lungs and make him more susceptible to disease.

- Have smoke and $CO_2$ detectors in your basement and in the hallways near bedrooms.

- Place guards in front of open fire-places, heaters, steam radiators, hot air registers, floor furnaces, and riser pumps. Kerosene and space heaters, which can tip over, are very danger-ous.

- Keep firearms and ammunition locked up separately at all times.

- Remove sharp-edged furniture from your child's play area. Safety edges made of soft plastic are useful for covering sharp corners on coffee tables or other low furniture. Foam tape can cover the edges of glass tables.

- If your home's walls, windows, or doors are covered with paint made before 1977, consider repainting. These old paints contain lead that can be harmful, especially if your baby finds paint chips and puts them in his mouth.

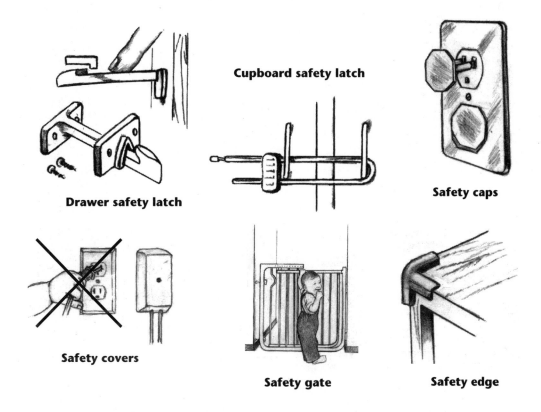

**Drawer safety latch**

**Cupboard safety latch**

**Safety caps**

**Safety covers**

**Safety gate**

**Safety edge**

## KITCHEN OR DINING ROOM

- Keep hazardous and poisonous substances (see list on pages 81–82) locked up or out of reach. Use drawer and cupboard safety latches to prevent your child from getting into areas that hold potentially dangerous objects.

- Make sure any garbage pails are inaccessible.

- Be very careful about letting your baby crawl or walk around the kitchen while you're cooking or serving meals. A baby sitting in a baby carrier on a counter may also be spattered by grease or food.

- Turn all pot handles inward so that your child can't pull them off the stove. A good policy while cooking is to simmer foods on the front burners and boil foods on the back burners.

- Never leave the oven door open. And keep your children away from oven doors that are hot to the touch.

- Don't let your child play with knobs on a gas stove. If necessary, remove the knobs.

- Don't drink hot liquids while your baby is in your lap. You might spill by accident, or the baby's moving arm might tip or knock hot liquid onto himself or you.

- Keep all objects and hot liquids out of your baby's reach and away from the edges of counters and tables.

- Avoid using tablecloths while your baby is small. Babies love to pull the edges, and they could pull things on top of themselves.

## BATHROOM

- Never leave your baby alone in the bathtub—not even for a second.

- Before bathing your baby, always check the bath water to make sure it's not too hot. Turn off the faucets tightly so that your baby can't open them. It's a good idea to set your hot water heater at 125°F (51.6°C) to eliminate any chance for your baby to be unintentionally scalded.

- Don't let your baby play in the bathroom; there are too many hard objects and slippery surfaces, and a curious child could drown in a toilet bowl. As a rule, keep the bathroom door closed.

- Never leave hot curling irons near your baby, as this is a common cause of burns. Unplug and put away hair dryers when they're not in use, especially if they're near water or a source of water.

- Put medicines and other potentially hazardous materials—cleansers, cosmetics, and soaps—away immediately after use (see list on pages 81–82). If the phone rings while you are using such a substance, ignore the call or take the child with you to answer the phone.

- Buy medicine in childproof containers.

- Always check medicine labels for proper dosages before administering them to your child. Never give medicine to a child in a darkened room. Don't give medicine prescribed for one child to another child.

- Don't save leftover medications; safely discard any unused part of a prescription.

- Avoid calling the medicine "candy" so that the child doesn't associate the two. A leading cause of poisoning in children are overdoses of good-tasting medicine, such as candy-flavored vitamins and aspirin.

## BEDROOM

- Never leave a baby unattended on a changing table, bed, couch, or other high place from which it's possible to fall. While changing your baby, use a safety strap or keep one hand on him at all times. If the phone rings while you're changing the baby, or if you must leave the room, wrap him up and take him with you or lay him down in a crib or playpen.

- Buy only flame-retardant sleepwear, generally polyester, for your baby.

- When your baby is able to sit up alone, lower the crib mattress. Set it at its lowest point before the baby can stand.

- Don't leave large toys in a crib or playpen. The baby can use them as steps to climb up and out.

- Place humidifiers, vaporizers, and portable heaters beyond your child's reach, and keep them away from your child's bedclothes.

- Consider putting a sticker on your baby's window that would alert a firefighter to the presence of a child in that room, and make an escape plan for your family in case of fire.

## STAIRS

- Keep stairs free of objects that could cause you to fall while carrying your baby. Remove extension cords and scatter rugs. Hold the handrail while going up or down stairs. Don't wax stairs.

- When your baby starts to move around, you should barricade tops and bottoms of staircases with safety gates. Babies learn to go up before they learn to go down. Make sure your gates are wall-mounted, not pressure-mounted and that no gaps in them are more than one-and-a-half inches wide.

## OUTSIDE

- Don't allow your infant in the yard when you are using power equipment, such as lawn mowers or snow blowers.

- Never leave your infant alone outside; he could crawl or walk into the street.

- When you're outdoors, watch to make sure your baby doesn't pick up dangerous objects or put them in his mouth.

- Be careful about exposing your baby to direct sunlight. Build up your child's exposure first. In the beginning, two minutes of sun a day should be the maximum. Gradually increase the exposure time until after a month it equals forty-five minutes. Try not to expose your baby to midday sun. The safest time to be in the sun is before 10 A.M. and after 3 P.M. A good sun block (SPF 15 or more) will protect your baby's delicate skin against harmful rays.

- If you have a swimming pool, make sure there's a fence around it. Never leave a baby unsupervised in or near a pool.

## POISONOUS AND TOXIC SUBSTANCES

Here are some tips on avoiding or handling an accidental poisoning in your home:

- Make sure the number of the local poison-control center is posted near your telephones.

- Keep syrup of ipecac on hand; it's used to induce vomiting for some types of poisoning. However, always check with your poison-control center before using it. (See page 150.)

- All poisonous substances should be kept out of your child's reach, preferably in a locked container or cupboard. Use drawer safety latches, cupboard safety latches, or strapping tape to prevent access to potentially dangerous substances. And make sure you keep those drawers and cupboards closed, or the safety latches will do no good.

- Keep all hazardous materials and medicines in their original containers, with their original labels.

- When discarding containers that have held hazardous substances, put them in the garbage with a secure lid or remove them from the house altogether. An empty bottle of cleaner thrown into an accessible wastebasket is easy prey for a crawling baby.

- Don't let your baby chew on newspaper, magazine, or book pages. Some newsprint may be toxic.

- Children love to unwrap presents, but don't let them chew on the ribbons. The dye in some ribbons may be toxic.

- Don't let your child chew on window sills, porch steps, bars on iron gates, or any other surfaces that may have been painted with lead paint. When painting indoor surfaces and toys, use unaltered lead-free paint.

- Because children tend to imitate adults, don't take medicine in front of them.

Below is a list of household products and other substances that are potentially poisonous. This is only a general list. Many other substances, such as cosmetics, perfume, and mouthwash may be poisonous as well.

- Aspirin and other drugs
- Liquid furniture and auto polish
- Leaded paint
- Oil of wintergreen
- Cleaning fluids and powders
- Ammonia
- Bleach
- Metal polish
- Mothballs
- Shoe polish
- Insecticides
- Kerosene, gasoline, and benzene
- Insect and rat poisons
- Lye and alkalies for cleaning drains, bowls, and ovens
- Plant sprays and weed killers
- Detergents
- Washing soda
- Wax remover
- Borax
- Lighter fluid
- Turpentine
- Paint thinner
- Car cleaner
- Antifreeze

## POISONOUS PLANTS

Many household and garden plants are poisonous. Teach your baby never to eat or suck on any part of a plant not commonly used as food. Nibbling on leaves, sucking on plant stalks, or drinking water where plants have been may poison him. Below is a list of poisonous plants; some parts or all of these plants may be poisonous.

- Dieffenbachia
- Caladium
- Some philodendrons
- Poinsettia
- Holly berries
- Swedish ivy
- Lily of the valley
- Rhododendron
- Deadly nightshade
- Oleander
- Elephant ears
- Bulbs from hyacinth, narcissus, and daffodils
- Ivy
- Hydrangea
- Laurel
- Yew

# Baby Equipment

The following pages review the most common and helpful baby products, including information on what to look for when buying the equipment and how to use the products properly. Read *Consumer Reports* for more information on product safety and quality.

## CAR SEAT

As noted earlier, auto collisions are the most common cause of injuries or death in childhood. "Child-restraining devices" are required by law for children less than forty pounds or four years of age. It is illegal for children to ride without car seats. And the law makes sense: safely constructed and properly anchored restraints have been shown to reduce the probability of a fatal injury in auto accidents by well over 95 percent.

When a car hits another object or stops suddenly, all the occupants continue to move forward at the same speed at which the car was traveling—until something stops them. Unrestrained children become flying projectiles. Don't imagine you can protect your baby by holding him snugly in your arms. Even if you are strapped in, tests have shown that your baby would be torn from your arms by the force of an impact. And if you strap in your infant with your strap, your own weight, increased by the crash forces, can press the belt deeply into the

child's body and thereby cause serious or fatal injuries.

Children need to have crash forces spread evenly over their fragile bodies, which is exactly what car seats are designed to do. Most hospitals will not allow you to drive your baby home if you do not have an adequate car seat. Babies used to riding in a safety device from infancy will continue to accept restraint as a matter of course.

Here's what you need to know about car seats and auto travel with infants:

- Child-restraint seats must be installed and used exactly as recommended by the manufacturer. Seats not secured firmly enough in a car will not provide adequate protection. Some seats can be used only for infants or toddlers, while others can be converted for dual use.

- Infants weighing less than twenty pounds (9 kg) should ride in a semireclined, backward-facing restraint anchored to the seat by a lap belt. In case of an accident, the baby's sturdy back, rather than his delicate chest and abdomen, absorbs the crash forces.

- Do not place a rear-facing infant safety seat in a passenger seat equipped with an air bag. The bag's release on impact can seriously injure or kill a baby.

- Babies who are old enough to sit alone and weigh about twenty pounds (9 kg)—often at nine or ten months of age—can be moved to a forward-facing position in the car seat.

- The back seat is safer than the front seat, and the center of the vehicle is safer than the sides.

- It's not a good idea to buy an infant safety seat made before 1981. Make sure there is a label showing it meets all federal Motor Vehicle Safety Standards. Be wary of buying used seats; there is no way to know whether they have been damaged in an accident.

- Don't carry heavy or loose objects unsecured inside a vehicle, and don't let your children play with pens, pencils, or other sharp or metal objects while the car is moving.

- Never leave a child unattended in a car. The inside of a car can get quite stuffy in hot weather, and a child who is old enough could unintentionally set the car in motion.

- Do not use infant seats in a boat. They don't float.

## CRIB

Because your baby spends so much time in it—much of it unattended—possibly no piece of home baby equipment is as important as the crib. New Consumer Product Safety Commission regulations about cribs went into effect in 1974. Make sure any crib you buy, new or used, meets these standards, described as follows:

- The space between crib bars must be two-and-three-eighths inches (5.9 cm) or less—roughly the width of three adult fingers—so that your baby's head can't get caught between them. Be careful of loose bars that could come out, leaving dangerous gaps. Make or buy a crib bumper to tie around the inside perimeter of the crib.

- The mattress should be the same size as the crib so your baby can't get wedged between the mattress and the crib sides. If you can fit two fingers between the mattress and side of the crib, the mattress is too small. Until you can replace it with a larger mattress, stuff large towels or blankets between the mattress and sides of the crib.

- The minimum height from the top of the railing to a mattress set at the lowest level should be twenty-two inches (55 cm).

- When lowered, sides should be four inches (10 cm) above the mattress. Sides should be operated with a locking, hand-operated latch that can't be easily or accidentally released.

- Metal hardware should be smooth— no rough edges or exposed bolts.

- If you paint your crib, use a lead-free, nontoxic paint.

- When the height of the crib side is less than three-quarters of your child's height, it's a good time to move him to a bed to decrease his chance of falling out.

## STROLLER OR CARRIAGE

- Strollers and baby carriages should have safety belts to prevent a child from standing up and to keep his weight properly centered.

- Look for a wide wheel base and wheels that are large in diameter.

- On a folding stroller, see that there is an adequate lock to prevent accidental collapse. Look for the safety catch.

- Check to be sure that there are no sharp edges or scissor-like mechanisms.

- Make sure there's enough headroom when the canopy is down so your baby won't outgrow the stroller too quickly.

- Don't hang bags on stroller handles. They could cause the stroller to tilt.

## BACKPACK

A backpack is a great way to carry your baby, either outside or in the house. But don't use one before your baby is four to five months old, when his neck will be strong enough to withstand jolts.

- Choose a carrier to match your baby's size. Leg openings should be neither so big that the baby could slip through nor so small that legs become chafed. There should be enough depth to support the baby's back. Many models have adjustable straps and an inner seat.

- Look for a carrier made of sturdy material, with strong stitching and heavy-duty snaps. Also look for a padded covering over the metal frame near the baby's face.

- Make sure there are no joints that may close, pinch, or cut your baby. See that there are no sharp points or edges, and no rough surfaces.

- Always use safety straps.

- When leaning over or stooping, bend from your knees, not from your waist, so the baby doesn't fall out.

## INFANT SEAT

- Look for a wide base for stability.

- Check supporting devices that snap on the back of a baby carrier. Some can pop out, causing the carrier to collapse.

- Never use a baby carrier as a car seat (but you can use a car seat as a baby carrier). Stay within arm's reach of your baby when the carrier is on a table, counter, couch, chair, or other high place. Avoid putting it on slippery surfaces, such as glass tabletops.

- You may want to avoid putting your baby in an infant seat directly after a feeding, as his stomach won't empty as well. (See burping and spitting up, page 68.)

- Always use a safety strap while the baby is in a carrier. If the carrier doesn't have one, attach your own.

## FRONT CARRIER

A soft front carrier is a wonderful way to transport your new baby. Your baby will enjoy the warm containment it provides, and you'll like the freedom it gives you to move about, both indoors and outdoors.

- Make sure the carrier is made of strong fabric and has well-constructed seams, padded leg holes, and padded shoulder straps.

- Be sure there is no way for a baby to slip through the side or leg openings.

## HIGHCHAIR

Once your infant starts to eat solid foods and can sit up without support—usually between six and eight months—you'll be using a highchair regularly.

- Buy a chair with an adjustable tray and footrest to adapt to the baby's growth.

- Choose a wide base for stability. Also, make sure that the highchair has a safety strap that is not attached to the tray, and always use it. Make sure the safety straps go between your baby's legs so that it's impossible for the baby to slide down through the chair.

- Avoid hardware with rough edges or sharp points.

- Check the tray to see that it is properly latched to both sides. The tray should have a strong tray latch.

- Supervise the child in the chair closely. Don't let other children pull on the chair or climb on it when the baby is in it, and don't allow a child to climb in or out of the seat alone.

- Situate the chair in an area free of traffic—away from doorways, refrigerators, ranges, and other equipment.

## PLAYPEN

A playpen (or play yard) can be useful when you want to put your child in a safe place so you can run to answer the door. But don't overuse it, because your baby needs to be able to explore. A playpen shouldn't be a substitute for a properly child-proofed house.

- If the playpen is wooden, make sure the side slats are set close together so that the baby's head can't get caught between them. Slats should be no more than two-and-three-eighths inches (5.9 cm) apart.

- If the playpen is mesh, check openings in the netting to see that they aren't wide enough for the baby's arms and legs to poke through and get caught. Playpens that have small-weave netting are preferable.

- See that any metal catches are outside the mesh or railing. Also, any mesh models should have a padded rim.

- Make sure that hinges and latches on folding models lock tightly. There should be no scissoring action when the playpen is in use.

- Check for firm floor support to prevent a playpen's legs from collapsing.

- Keep the playpen away from potentially dangerous objects—lamps, cords, glass, blinds, stoves, and heaters, for example. Don't tie toys to playpen railings. A string could get caught around a child's neck.

## NURSERY MONITOR

A nursery monitor is useful in alerting parents to their waking baby. Positioned in the nursery, a transmitter unit sends sounds to parents listening in on a portable receiver in another room.

## JUMP-UP HARNESS AND WIND-UP SWING

- Read the instructions for hanging the jump-up carefully; if it's not secured properly, it could come loose while the baby is inside.

- The swing should be sturdy and have no loose screws or bolts. The seat and crossbar should be strong and well-constructed to prevent the baby from falling forward.

- Check for potentially dangerous springs that might injure your baby's fingers.

- Position the swing or harness away from traffic areas in the home and away from potentially dangerous objects that a baby might reach for, such as electrical appliances, heaters, and glasses.

- Check leg and side openings to make sure that a baby can't slip through them.

- A baby in a wind-up swing or harness should be supervised at all times. Babies have been known to tip them over.

## A WORD ABOUT WALKERS AND BICYCLE SEATS

The American Academy of Pediatrics has recommended a ban on infant walkers, and Canada has already banned walkers. Even if you find a walker with a wide base and a frame that doesn't pinch fingers or toes, it will not prevent a baby from rolling into a stairwell or a hot stove. The devices may even impede the progress of a baby learning to crawl or walk, according to the Academy.

Bicycle seats are not recommended for babies during the first year. It's best not to take babies on a bicycle ride at all during this time, as it is too jarring.

# Babysitters

You'll no doubt use the services of a babysitter at some time during your child's first year. Even if you leave your baby at daycare during the week, you'll probably be nervous the first few times you leave your baby with someone else for an evening or weekend outing. To help ease your mind, make sure any babysitter you hire has had experience and feels comfortable with small babies. Observe how your sitter handles the baby, and give your baby time to become comfortable with your sitter.

Here's some other general, common-sense advice about babysitters:

- Always leave the phone numbers where you can be reached and the time you'll be home. Preprinted forms can help you organize this information. If you can't be reached, check in periodically and leave the phone number of someone the sitter could contact in case of an emergency. Check with that person ahead of time to make sure he or she will be home.

- Show the sitter where you keep the phone numbers of your doctor, hospital, ambulance, police, and poison-control center.

- Check whether the sitter knows what to do in case of emergencies, such as falls, choking, and fire. Have a first-aid chart handy for the sitter to refer to in case of an accident. Show the locations of your fire exits. Review these procedures with the sitter, just to make sure. If the sitter does not know, instruct him or her carefully.

- When using a babysitter for the first time, it's a good idea to have him or her come early (or the day before) so you can review safety procedures.

- Inform the sitter of any allergies your child may have. If the sitter needs to administer medicine to the child, be sure he or she knows the correct dosage and knows not to give medicine to the child in a darkened room.

- Inform your sitter of any special precautions that should be taken with the baby.

# Traveling

As members of extended families move further from each other geographically, more and more parents find themselves traveling with a baby. Mostly, it will be in a car, but you may even have occasion to take an airplane ride with your child.

The best things you can do to keep your baby quiet and content for any trip are to dress him appropriately and bring along toys, snacks, and plenty of diapers. In a car, also remember that you'll need to stop more often than you otherwise would. The key is to plan ahead while staying flexible.

Following are some tips that can keep your baby safe and comfortable while traveling in an airplane:

- Children under two are considered lap babies, meaning that they can fly for free on your lap. This practice is not a safe one. Should you decide to travel without buying a ticket for your baby to ride in a separate seat, do not strap him into the seatbelt with you. Strap yourself in firmly and hold onto the baby. Bring your child restraint seat along with you; airlines will generally let you use it in an empty seat. Also, make sure you don't ride in a row with another lap baby. In case of an emergency, there is only one extra oxygen mask for each row.

- For the airport, you'll find that an umbrella-type stroller, which can fold up and fit in an overhead compartment, is a great convenience.

- Tell the ticket agent that you're traveling with a baby so that you will not be placed in an emergency exit row.

- Give your baby a bottle or pacifier during takeoff and landing. Sucking and swallowing will equalize pressure in the ears.

- Plan your meals. Baby food is sometimes available on airplanes, but you may be better off bringing your own. To warm a bottle, put it in an airsickness bag filled with hot water.

- Changing diapers will be a challenge. Put dirty diapers in airsickness bags and dispose of them in the bathroom trash.

# CHAPTER 5

# Your Baby's Development

The first year of life is an exciting time for parents. You watch and help as your child gradually changes from a helpless newborn, controlled by instincts, reflexes, and basic survival needs, to a toddler with a distinct personality. Toddlers will actively explore, communicate, solve problems, and begin to become independent in many ways. The first year is a time of rapid change for your child and your family, with new experiences taking place and new skills developing nearly every day.

Your child is an individual; no one else is quite the same. Although children develop within the same general sequence, each child's timing is unique. Your baby will spurt ahead in one area of development, while standing still in others; then she'll catch up in these areas, while practicing and perfecting the earlier skills. The milestones of development presented in the following pages are only meant to suggest what a typical pattern of development might be. Do not be alarmed if your infant strays from this pattern during the first year.

All children have a drive to learn, to explore, and to grow. All they need is a safe, loving, interesting environment with as few limitations as possible on their activity. As they mature, their tools for learning will change, and their skills will increase in complexity. Formal teaching is seldom necessary at this stage. The activities that infants undertake, the games they naturally play, and eventually their imitation of the people around them serve as tools for learning and surviving.

Enjoy watching your child. Observe her preferences, cues, responses, and early attempts to initiate interaction. Try often to see the world from her perspective and respond to her cues.

# Birth Through Two Months

Basic physical and emotional needs dominate life for the first two months. At first it seems that babies only eat and sleep. Awake or asleep, most movements are in relation to the reflexes discussed in the first chapter. During brief periods of alertness, infants begin to use basic senses—one sense at a time—to learn about themselves and their surroundings. The inability of an infant this age to control her movements severely limits this exploration.

At this age, your baby does not know that there are objects or people separate from herself. Everything is part of her world. The basis for your baby's future confidence, relationships, trust in the world, and even independence is now developing. She learns gradually that her needs are met regularly and lovingly, that her world is a safe, secure, fairly predictable place. This sense of security will eventually enable her to try new things, to feel comfortable in an unfamiliar place, and to continue to grow and develop in all ways.

## DURING THE FIRST MONTH, YOUR BABY MAY . . .

- make movements that are mostly caused by reflexes; for instance, grasping or stepping. (See page 17.)

- lift her head briefly when lying on her stomach; otherwise, she can't hold it up without support.

- make eye-to-eye contact at close range, usually between eight to twelve inches (20 to 30 cm).

- stare at objects (without reaching for them) and prefer looking at faces and patterns—contrasting colors, such as red and yellow or black and white, seem to be infants' favorite visual stimulation.

- sleep a lot and be alert for only brief spells each day.

- begin to be comforted by mouthing and sucking the fist and fingers.

- show enjoyment by quieting down and possibly producing a short-lived smile.

- distinguish one or two people by their voices.

## DURING THE SECOND MONTH, YOUR BABY MAY . . .

- turn from side to side, so that if you're not careful, your baby could roll off a bed or table.

- lie in the "fencing" position—one arm straight out, head turned to that side, and the other arm flexed up.

- have better head control. While sitting, your baby may hold her head up unsteadily; lying on her stomach, she may hold it up for a few minutes.

- prefer sleeping on or looking to one particular side.

- begin to control her grasp and hold an object for a few minutes.

- use only one sense at a time—that is, sucking in bursts, looking during pauses.

- prefer looking at faces or moving objects and people, but focus only on close objects.

- begin to follow some movements with her eyes.

- begin to seek and respond to attention by smiling, making sounds, and moving the arms and legs actively.

- cry at predictable intervals, make cooing sounds, and generally be interested in sounds.

- recognize her mother's voice and handling.

- associate some positions and people with certain events—for instance, her mother with feeding.

# Three Through Five Months

As periods of alertness increase in length and frequency, babies become dramatically more active. Your baby is gradually learning to grasp objects purposefully and bring them up to her face to look at and taste. She is discovering the characteristics of each object through sensory exploration, especially mouthing. Developing the ability to sit when supported frees an infant's hands and increases the field of vision, which allows her to investigate her surroundings more fully.

Your baby's social awareness is blossoming as she seeks and acknowledges attention by smiling, making noises, and moving her whole body. It is clear that she is becoming more interested in the people and objects around her and that she is enjoying her own activity as well as that of others.

## DURING THE THIRD MONTH, YOUR BABY MAY . . .

- rest on her forearms when lying on her stomach and holding her head up.

- sit supported for a few minutes.

- begin to reach for an object with both hands, bat at things, and kick with force.

- explore a room visually for light colors, shapes, and patterns, and search for the source of a sound.

- smile spontaneously.

- look and suck at the same time.

- be attentive up to three-quarters of an hour at a time.

- begin to show memory of sequences, effects, and people.

- use a variety of movements and expressions to indicate moods and needs.

- make sounds in response to talking and singing.

## DURING THE FOURTH MONTH, YOUR BABY MAY . . .

- roll from back to side or from stomach to side or back.

- sit supported, with head steady, for ten to fifteen minutes.

- push herself straight up from her stomach.

- look at and play with her own hands.

- reach for (and possibly miss), grasp, hold, and release objects with her hand.

- put everything in her mouth.

- splash in the bath.

- turn her head and eyes to look in all directions, watch moving adults, or locate the source of a sound.

- begin babbling and practicing sounds.

- laugh.

- become attached to one object or toy.

- discriminate among faces and know her mother.

- be alert for at least one hour at a time and have sustained interest in detail.

- anticipate a feeding with increased activity and enjoy eating as a social and play time; she may not require a night feeding.

## DURING THE FIFTH MONTH, YOUR BABY MAY . . .

- move by rocking, rolling (from stomach to back or back to side), twisting, and kicking.

- sit propped with back firm, for up to half an hour.

- be easily pulled to a stand.

- reach for and grasp an object smoothly.

- wave and raise arms in anticipation of being picked up, and cling when held.

- bring her feet to her mouth and suck on her toes.

- make sounds to herself, her toys, or her mirror image, and babble to get attention.

- show fear, disgust, or anger by making sounds.

- awaken at dawn, ready and eager to play.

- be alert for one or two hours at a time, resisting interruptions in play.

# Six Through Nine Months

Infants significantly enlarge their world when they begin to propel themselves from place to place by rolling, creeping, and eventually crawling. A baby who is allowed to move freely in a baby-proofed environment will begin to investigate the home. Few objects will escape your child's insatiable curiosity. She is beginning to experiment, moving and looking at things in different ways, squeezing, poking, and still tasting everything.

Increasingly, your baby is learning not only by doing, but by watching and imitating others. She will remember that parents exist, even when they're out of sight. And she is beginning to perceive and respond to others' mood swings.

As tiny as she seems, in many ways, your baby is already starting to become an independent person, with a separate personality and distinct likes and dislikes. She is also starting to move away from the comfort of a caretaker's lap, and even to feed herself.

## DURING THE SIXTH MONTH, YOUR BABY MAY . . .

- roll from back to stomach.

- sit unsupported for a short time, with her head well balanced and her hands free.

- love to stand, with lots of support, and bounce.

- begin to drop things from the high-chair, look for them, and cry for others to pick them up.

- transfer toys from hand to hand and rotate wrists to turn and manipulate toys.

- want to handle all food and utensils.

- repeat combinations of sounds ("da-da-da"), watch mouths closely, and try to imitate inflections.

- show enjoyment of music by humming, swaying, or bouncing.

- babble; varying pitch, volume, and speed.

- watch and play with a brother or sister.

- remember that her mother exists even when not in the room.

- show her own individual style in activity level, amount of sleep required, and food preferences.

## DURING THE SEVENTH MONTH, YOUR BABY MAY . . .

- creep on her stomach—first backward, then forward—and try to crawl.

- explore her own body parts.

- carry a toy most of the time.

- love noise-making objects; your child may bang blocks on the floor or shake things, for example.

- say several syllables and use different ones in the same breath, such as "ma," "mu," "da," and "bah."

- want to be included socially.

- show increasing dependence and fear of separation; fear strangers.

- show tension and irritability before a big developmental step like sitting or crawling.

- dislike having a familiar toy removed and resist pressure to do something she doesn't want to do.

- want to help in feeding. Your child will explore foods with her hands, smear them into her mouth, close her lips on a spoon to remove food, and hold a cup and spoon.

## DURING THE EIGHTH MONTH, YOUR BABY MAY . . .

- crawl.

- learn to pull herself to a standing position, discovering which furniture is stable in the process.

- get into a sitting position, and use her hands to get herself up.

- empty cabinets, drawers, and book-shelves.

- push away unwanted objects.

- put an object into a container and shake it.

- pick up a small object with her thumb and two forefingers.

- hold a bottle to drink.

- babble with a variety of sounds, inflections, and two-syllable utterances; she may shout for attention.

- listen selectively to familiar words and begin to recognize some.

- repeat sounds or movements she has already made.

- respond to cues of upcoming events; for instance, your child may blink before a cup hits the floor or cry when parents put on their coats to leave.

- solve simple problems, such as pulling a string to get the toy that's attached.

- resist bedtimes and naps.

## DURING THE NINTH MONTH, YOUR BABY MAY . . .

- stand briefly, while you hold her hand.

- sit steadily alone and pivot a quarter of the way around.

- grasp a small object with her thumb and forefinger, in pincer fashion.

- put her fingers into holes.

- pass an object from one hand to the other.

- be able to finger-feed herself bits of food and drink from a cup with help.

- understand and respond to one or two words other than her name, and be able to carry out simple commands, such as "no-no," "wave," "clap," or "get me the . . . ."

- look with interest at pictures in a book.

- perform for home audiences and repeat actions if applauded or laughed at.

- prefer watching children to watching adults.

- begin to show persistence.

- enjoy nursery games such as pat-a-cake and peekaboo, respond to them, and remember a game from the previous day.

- fear bathing, heights, and separation from her mother in a strange place.

- begin to evaluate and respond to others' moods.

# Ten Through Twelve Months

These months are a time of transition for children as they begin the change from infants to toddlers and from babblers to talkers. Your baby is just beginning to learn rules of acceptable and safe behavior and seek social approval. Gradually refining the use of her hands allows her to use other objects as tools.

The imitation of actions and sounds is developing into the imitation of words, as your baby begins to bring the level of the words she can say up to the level of the words she can understand. Your baby's self-confidence and assertiveness grow as she acquires more self-help skills. She is on her way to becoming a fully functioning, competent, self-assured person.

**DURING THE TENTH MONTH, YOUR BABY MAY . . .**

- stand, for a few moments, with little support.

- cruise along furniture.

- climb on chairs.

- walk with help.

- lift her leg to help in dressing.

- carry an object in each hand and dangle an object from a string.

- hold and bite a cookie, finger-feed herself an entire meal.

- say "dada" and "mama," though she may not understand them as specific names.

- understand and obey some simple commands.

- imitate non-speech sounds, such as coughs and tongue clicks.

- imitate actions, remember them, and repeat them later.

- remember where unseen toys are.

- become self-conscious and sensitive to social approval or disapproval.

- develop a sense of identity and possession and show tenderness to stuffed animals and other toys.

## DURING THE ELEVENTH MONTH, YOUR BABY MAY . . .

- walk, holding onto one or two hands.

- stand much of the time, without assistance.

- climb up stairs, but have trouble coming down.

- use two hands at the same time for different functions; for instance, she may support herself while picking up a toy.

- experiment with dropping and picking up objects.

- try the same activity with each hand or with each side of her body.

- help more actively in dressing—pulling off a sock, putting her foot in a shoe.

- hold a cup with both hands and bring a spoon to her mouth.

- explore containers by lifting their lids and putting objects in and taking them out while looking inside.

- understand much more than she can say.

- mix a word into her babbling or use one word to express a whole thought.

- be very dependent on her mother, imitate family members constantly, and play actively with her father.

- be shy with strangers and play alongside, but not with, another child.

- resist and test limits and seek approval.

## DURING THE TWELFTH MONTH, YOUR BABY MAY . . .

- walk with a wide-legged gait, but may prefer crawling.

- get to a standing position from a squat, pivot a quarter of the way around, and lower herself to a sitting position.

- use one hand more than the other in reaching, thumb-sucking, and finger-feeding; she may use a spoon and spill often.

- hold a crayon to make marks.

- push cars and balls and give a toy to an adult on request.

- bang toys or objects together.

- stack blocks.

- cooperate in getting dressed.

- use trial and error to solve problems.

- turn into a very picky eater and become more negative, especially at meals and naptime.

- give affection to people and objects.

- have renewed fear of strangers and strange situations.

# Toys for the First Year

To an infant and toddler, everything is a toy. Fingers and toes, crib rungs, buttons and strings on clothing, people and pets, household objects, and even pieces of lint are toys. A child's play is her work. Her task is to learn about herself and her world, and her toys are the materials with which she learns.

Because your child will play with anything within reach (and things you thought were out of reach), it is your job to be sure that her reachable world is as safe as possible. (See Chapter 4 on this subject.) It is also up to you to offer appropriate new challenges for your baby. The right toys are ones that will be interesting at your child's current developmental level—not too difficult or frustrating and not too limited or simple. The charts on the following pages are designed to help you provide toys that fit your child's developmental abilities.

This doesn't mean that you must buy lots of expensive toys. Many parents, in fact, are discouraged to find that their children prefer to play with the boxes that toys come in rather than the toys themselves. You can provide your infant with nearly everything she needs by making toys at home or by simply allowing common household objects to become playthings.

- You can suspend some colorful pictures from a clothes hanger to make a mobile. (Make sure any strings or cords are secured tightly.)

- When your baby starts to play with her own feet, you can sew bells onto her shoes or booties.

- A set of unbreakable mixing bowls or plastic containers for dropping things into and dumping things out of fascinates all babies.

- You can make a simple "clacking" toy by stringing a number of empty wooden thread spools together.

Following are some considerations you should be aware of, whether you make or buy toys for your child.

## SAFETY

Toys and movable parts of toys must be large enough to prevent your child from swallowing them. Pieces must not pull or break off or be able to be chewed off, and toys should not have sharp points or edges. Materials should be labeled nontoxic.

## DURABILITY

Toys should not break under the kind of abuse your child can and will give them.

## VERSATILITY

A particularly good toy will have many uses at many different ages or developmental levels. There will be more than one right way to use it. Good toys also stimulate more than one sense. For example, some clutch toys now on the market are brightly colored, have faces to look at, are easy to hold, have interesting textures to touch and mouth, and have a bell inside to stimulate hearing and encourage shaking or turning. Few, if any, toys appeal to all the senses, but many appeal to more than one.

| TOY | AGE | DEVELOPMENTAL ACTIVITY |
|---|---|---|
| **Pictures** | From birth on | Use pictures to aid the development of your child's visual perception (including focus, distance, detail, color, and image recognition). Attach brightly colored decals, posters, or other pictures—especially pictures of faces—to the crib, the wall, or a mobile. At first your baby will focus eight to twelve inches (20 to 30 cm) away; by four to six months she will be able to focus across the room. |
| **Mobile** | Birth to 2 months | A mobile will engage your infant's active interest in her surroundings, especially bright colors and shapes. Look at the mobile from your baby's perspective and place it five to eighteen inches (12 to 45 cm) from her face. |
| | 3 to 6 months | At this stage, your child will reach for and grasp her mobile, thus learning to coordinate hand movements by looking at the target. Move the mobile around so your baby can use her feet as well as her hands to kick, bat, pull, and push it. If the toy makes a noise when your baby moves it or kicks the mattress, she'll be even more interested. Always remove mobiles once your baby can stand. |
| **Mirror** | 2 to 6 months, and beyond | A mirror helps your child develop an interest in faces and foster the idea that faces are part of people and that she is a separate person. Hang a small, good-quality, unbreakable mirror on the inner side of the crib, over your baby's head in the crib, or next to the changing table. Your baby will enjoy watching and talking to herself and will later look at any of the mirrors you have in the house. |

| TOY | AGE | DEVELOPMENTAL ACTIVITY |
|---|---|---|
| **Stuffed animals** | 2 months on | Stuffed animals stimulate lots of activities: an interest in faces (2 months); reaching and grasping (3 to 6 months); and early manipulation of objects and interest in textures (6 to 18 months). A young infant may become attracted to a stuffed animal because of its face. Primarily it's something soft to reach for, grasp, and mouth. Do not leave stuffed animals in your baby's crib. Sleeping next to one can cause a baby to breathe in carbon dioxide instead of oxygen. |
| | 4 months on | Your child may become attached to a toy by showing affection for it. A baby will quickly sense what is important to her parents. Because we often hug, talk to, or pay more attention to a stuffed animal than to other toys, your baby may become more attached to this type of toy than to others. |
| **Rattle/squeak toy** | 2 to 4 months | Rattles, squeak toys, or anything with bells on it give your infant a chance to watch a moving object and look for the source of the sound. Move a brightly colored, shiny rattle or squeak toy slowly past your baby's eyes. She will move only her eyes at first, then her head, too. Gently shake the rattle or squeak the toy in front of her, then to each side. Your baby will learn to look for the source of the sound. |
| | 3 to 7 months | As she gets older, rattles or squeak toys can help your child develop her ability to reach, grasp, and release. She'll learn to handle, shake, and bang toys. Hold or suspend the toy where your baby can reach it. Experiment by putting it in front of or to each side of your baby. |

| TOY | AGE | DEVELOPMENTAL ACTIVITY |
|-----|-----|------------------------|
| **Cradle gym or exerciser** | 3 to 6 months | A cradle gym, which you string over the top of your baby's crib or hang over your baby when she is lying on her back on the floor, will provide a variety of objects to look at, pull, push, kick at, and grasp. |
| **Ball** | 3 to 4 months | A brightly colored ball with some kind of noise-making object inside is best at this age to give your child the chance to watch moving objects and look and reach for the source of a sound. Turn or roll the ball slowly in front of your baby. A soft clutch toy designed with places to hold onto is easy to grasp and shake. |
| | 4 months on | When your child has begun to roll over, creep, crawl, and finally walk, a ball that's small enough to be held in one hand will be turned, shaken, banged, dropped, rolled, and followed. Again, color and sound add interest. |
| **Stacking rings** | 3 to 6 months | The removable pieces from a stacking toy are usually brightly colored, easy to grasp, durable, and smooth to mouth. They're perfect objects for a young baby to reach for and handle. They can be strung as a mobile, hung from the side of the crib, or held out for a child to touch. |
| | 9 months on | Later, your child will actually use the rings as stacking objects and learn to control hand movements in order to place them precisely in one spot. At first your baby will make a stack of the pieces. When this is no longer a challenge, give her the post on which to stack the rings (with the pieces on it), take one off and put it back on. Your baby's curiosity will do the rest. |

| TOY | AGE | DEVELOPMENTAL ACTIVITY |
|-----|-----|------------------------|
| **Board books** | 6 months on | Your baby may not show much interest in books early on, but they can play a useful role in language development. Point to pictures, naming them and describing them as you go. Make animal sounds or tell stories, and by nine or ten months, your baby will certainly enjoy a book as an object, turning it over, pulling pages back and forth, mouthing it, and dropping it. Be sure books are sturdy or expendable, or both. |
| **Small blocks** | 5 to 6 months, and beyond | This is one of the most versatile, long-lasting toys you will find. Your child will learn to pick up and drop objects and coordinate hand movements by looking. A small, brightly colored block is easy to handle and see. Later, she will bang blocks together. She'll drop small objects into large containers and, eventually, enjoy the challenge of putting a block through a hole in the lid of the container. Even up to age five, your child can use blocks for building, dramatic play, and learning about size, shape, color, numbers, and so on. |
| **"Nesting" toys** | 5 to 10 months, and beyond | Nesting toys are objects of the same shape but different sizes (like cups, bowls, cubes, etc.) that can be nested, or fit, inside one another. Using them helps your child develop hand coordination and learn that objects exist when they're not visible. While she watches, use a cup to cover up a small toy that she likes, uncover it, and show her where it is. Your baby will soon play the game herself. |

| TOY | AGE | DEVELOPMENTAL ACTIVITY |
|-----|-----|------------------------|
| **Pull toys** | 8 months to 2½ years | When your baby can crawl, walk along furniture and finally walk alone, pull toys will give her a sense of power, specifically over objects, and an extra enjoyment about new modes of movement. However, most pull toys tip over readily, which frustrates children. Look for sturdy, stable toys, preferably those that are colorful or interesting to look at and make some sound as they move. |
| **Playpen activity box or cube** | 6 months to 1½ years | An activity box provides objects that can be manipulated, turned, pushed, poked, or hit. This kind of toy has a variety of gadgets, such as doors to open, balls to spin, and telephone dials to turn. |

# Baby Exercises

FOLLOWING are some things you can do to test your infant's reflexes. And though your baby will likely do enough moving around on her own, these excercises provide a muscular workout as well as fun playtime between parent and child. Remember to use discretion. Make sure your baby is developmentally ready, for example, when trying the Inchworm.

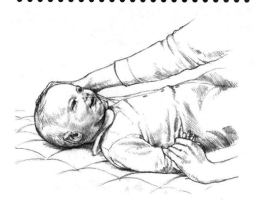

**1** THE GRASP (To elicit the grasp reflex.) Put your forefingers in your baby's palms. She will grasp your fingers. Gently pull her hand toward you, and she will pull back on your finger. (Do not attempt to raise her head and shoulders up.) Pat and bounce her hands if they are closed in a fist.

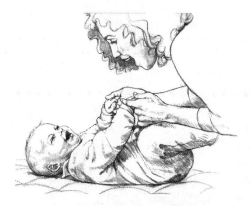

**2** ARM CROSS (To relax the chest and upper back muscles.) Place your thumbs in the palms of your baby's hands; she will grasp them. Open her arms wide to the sides and then bring them together and cross her arms over her chest. Repeat slowly and gently, using rhythmic movements.

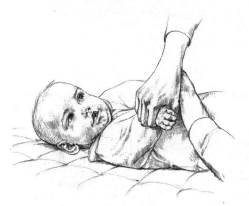

**3** ARM RAISING (To improve the flexibility of the shoulders.) Grasp your baby's forearms near the elbows. Raise them over her head, then lower them to the sides. Repeat slowly and gently, using rhythmic movements. Then alternate arms, so that one goes up while the other goes down.

# Baby Exercises

**4** LEG BENDING (To improve the flexibility of the hips; it may also help your baby pass gas.) With your baby on her back, grasp her lower legs and gently bend her knees up toward her abdomen and chest. Then gently lower her legs until they're straight. You may repeat this several times using both legs, or you may alternate, bending one leg while straightening the other.

**5** INCHWORM (To bring about the extension of the legs.) With your baby on her tummy, bend her knees under her and tuck her feet close to her body. Hold her feet with your thumbs against her soles. Press and wait. This pressure will cause your baby's legs to straighten, which moves her body forward like an inchworm. Curve your body slightly so your baby can fit comfortably next to you.

**6** BABY BOUNCE (To relax your baby's whole body.) Place your baby on her back or tummy on a very large, slightly deflated beach ball, a foam rubber pad, a bed, or any soft, bouncy surface. Slowly and gently press on the bouncy area around the baby so that she rocks up and down. Use a rhythmic pattern; as she feels the rhythmic up-and-down motion, she will relax. Also try patting your baby rhythmically on her stomach, chest, back, arms, and legs.

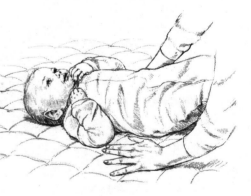

# CHAPTER 6

# Medical Care for Your Baby

**M**aking sure your infant is well cared for, both on a day-to-day basis and as an overall philosophy, helps to bring about a happy, less worrisome existence for both parent and child. And providing the basic building blocks for a physically and emotionally healthy child will reap benefits through an entire lifetime.

Taking your child in for a series of "well-child" checkups is one of the most important things you can do during this first year. Regular visits—when your infant is healthy—will help diminish the number of visits needed for illness or injury. Furthermore, a health care provider who can see you and your infant on a regular basis stands a better chance of being able to pick up on any changes or deviations in normal growth, development, or behavior, and thus catch problems early.

Being a parent is not always an easy job, especially if it's your first child.

Parenting certainly doesn't seem like a natural skill initially. Regular well-child visits give you the opportunity to share some of what you've experienced, what you've found challenging, and what puzzles you with a professional. The professional can help you in a number of ways—often just by reassuring you that what you're experiencing with your child is quite normal.

On the pages that follow, you'll find out more about the well-child checkups and immunizations recommended for the first year. There's also a section on the development of your child's teeth, a general discussion of how to handle common medical problems, and information on how to treat fever. The chapter concludes with step-by-step treatments for the illnesses and emergencies that your baby may face during his first year.

## CHECKUPS

In addition to being checked once or twice at the time of birth, your baby should have several routine examinations during the first year. In fact, the visits are more frequent during this year than during any other period, due both to an infant's many developmental changes and the need for immunization. The exact schedule may vary somewhat based on your individual health care provider and your baby's individual needs. Naturally, if your baby develops health problems that require further attention, you will see professionals more frequently. With earlier hospital discharge, babies generally need a checkup sooner than they did in past years.

A typical infant will go for a checkup sometime before he is two weeks old and again at two, four, six, nine, and twelve months of age. At nearly all of these checkups, a doctor or health care provider will:

- open a medical record and take a medical history or health profile;

- take measurements, such as height, weight, and head circumference;

- administer screening tests for vision, hearing, and anemia (by doing a hemoglobin test at approximately nine months);

- assess developmental and behavioral progress;

- discuss what to expect in your baby between the time of the checkup and the next visit with regard to nutrition, development, and safety.

Office visits are an ideal time to ask questions and share concerns about your baby. For the sake of fostering an open relationship with your health care provider and feeling comfortable, you should try to limit this care to one or two providers in a consistent setting, if possible. This way, you can see your baby's measurements plotted on a growth chart and discuss development. The physical examination will include using a stethoscope to listen to your baby's heart and lungs, an otoscope to look into the ears, and a light source to check the eyes and mouth. Your health care provider should also check the abdomen, genitals, hips, and legs.

## IMMUNIZATIONS

If you take your child in for the recommended well-child checkups, you'll also be making sure immunizations are a part of your child's health care. During the first year, your child will be immunized against at least six major diseases, including hepatitis B, polio, diphtheria, pertussis (whooping cough), tetanus, and haemophilus (Hib) infection. A single vaccine immunizes against the last four diseases. It requires an injection, usually into the upper thigh, as does the hepatitis B vaccine. The polio vaccine is usually given orally, but may be given by injection as well. New vaccines are on the horizon—for diarrheal illness, for example. Researchers are also exploring ways to combine new and existing vaccines to try to decrease unnecessary trauma on infants from a high number of injections.

An immunization is a preparation of dead or weakened organisms. When it's introduced into your child's system, it produces immunity to a specific disease by causing the body to build up antibodies or resistance to the organisms. These antibodies provide protection, should your child be exposed to the disease in the future. In addition, your baby may have a test for tuberculosis—given as a skin injection—if there is any risk of exposure to this disease.

For a variety of reasons, some infants will have reactions to certain vaccines. The most common and usually quite harmless reactions are general fussiness, a slight

## RECOMMENDED IMMUNIZATION SCHEDULE*

The following schedule may vary slightly among individual clinics and practices.

| Disease | 0–2 months | 2 months | 4 months | 6 months |
|---|---|---|---|---|
| Hepatitis B | • | • | | • |
| DPT/Hib (available in a combined vaccine) | | • | • | • |
| Polio | | • | • | • |

*After the first year, your baby will also be immunized for other diseases, such as varicella (chicken pox), measles, mumps, and rubella (German measles). He should also receive additional doses of the vaccines given in the first year. These are called boosters because they raise the protection level against the diseases.

fever, and a sore leg at the site of the injection. These usually occur within twenty-four hours after the injection. You can treat the fever with medication. (See pages 113–115.) If your child's leg becomes sore and swollen, you'll want to take extra care when you move it, and you might even want to apply warm washcloths to the swollen area.

In rare cases, more significant side effects can occur. You should expect to receive a written form about these issues or discuss and sign a permission to administer the vaccines. It is important to remember that the benefits of the vaccines strongly outweigh the risks. However, if your infant has had a seizure, or has a nervous system disease, has a fever at the time the vaccine is to be given, or has had a serious reaction to a previous vaccine, discuss these risks with your health care provider prior to a decision to vaccinate.

It's a good idea to record the dates and types of immunizations your baby receives on a card; this documentation will be helpful when you fill out school forms and the like in the future.

## DENTAL CARE

Your child's first tooth could appear any time from three to twelve months of age, although six months is the average. The tooth may simply pop through with no warning, or your baby may signal its entrance through typical teething symptoms: drooling, fussing, chewing on nearly everything in sight, waking frequently at night, and generally seeming bothered by sore, throbbing gums. Some babies even refuse to nurse or take a bottle if their teething is especially troublesome. Each child responds differently. (See page 153 for more on teething.)

A few more teeth are also likely to erupt during the first year, and a full set will probably be in place by the time your child is three. The following table lists the

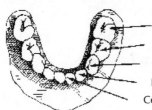

**Upper teeth**

Central incisors (8 to 12 months)

Lateral incisors (9 to 13 months)

Cuspids (16 to 22 months)

First molars (13 to 19 months)

Second molars (25 to 33 months)

**Lower teeth**

Second molars (23 to 31 months)

First molars (14 to 18 months)

Cuspids (17 to 23 months)

Lateral incisors (10 to 16 months)

Central incisors (6 to 10 months)

average times each baby, or primary, tooth erupts into the mouth. But don't worry if your child's teeth come in earlier or later.

Because healthy baby teeth are essential to the development of your baby's jaw and later permanent teeth, you should start caring for those first teeth even before they are visible.

- Make sure you provide a nutritious diet. Take your child out in the sunshine whenever it is practical, but don't forget the sunscreen. The sun is a natural source of vitamin D.

- A source of fluoride is recommended for babies beginning at six months of age. Most communities have fluoride added to the general water supply. But if you have well water, you will probably want to have it tested for fluoride levels. If your baby does not have access to fluoride you can provide it as a liquid supplement, available by prescription.

- Once your child is weaned from the breast or bottle, offer him plenty of foods rich in calcium, such as milk, cheese, and yogurt. Calcium is the primary mineral component of teeth.

- Try to avoid letting your child use the bottle as a pacifier, and don't put him to bed with it. Oftentimes, an older baby with this habit will demand several refills of milk or juice in a row, especially at night. This habit constantly bathes his teeth in sugary liquids and encourages decay because milk contains a form of sugar called lactose. If you feel you must give your baby a bottle in bed, make sure it contains water.

- The American Dental Association recommends that you start cleaning your child's teeth as soon as they appear. Use a sterile gauze pad or a clean washcloth to wipe the teeth, or gently brush them with a soft, small toothbrush, without toothpaste. This will clean away any harmful plaque that may have built up during the day.

## HANDLING COMMON MEDICAL PROBLEMS

When your infant is sick or hurt, you want to know quickly what's best to do. The step-by-step treatments on pages 118–156 will guide you as you care for your child and will indicate when professional help is necessary. These treatments cover the injuries, illnesses, and emergencies that your child may face at one time or another during that first year. You won't find a discussion, however, of diseases that are rare during this period, such as chicken pox.

The treatments in this section are medically sound, but they are not intended to replace professional medical care. Your own doctor may recommend other treatments for a number of reasons. Also, many illnesses vary in their symptoms and in their effects on different children. Not all issues are black and white, and not all illnesses can be diagnosed with accuracy at one visit. Children often need re-evaluation during the course of an illness to determine its severity. If you have any questions about your child's health or the best way to handle an illness or injury, please call your doctor's office for help or advice. The following symptoms are always worth at least a call to your health care provider's office:

1. Any clearly life-threatening injury or accident

2. Fever (see following guidelines)

3. Serious diarrhea

4. Blood in the urine or stools

5. Sudden loss of appetite that lasts four days or longer

6. Unusual crying

7. Difficulty breathing

8. Unusual vomiting

9. Off-color appearance, listlessness, or behavioral change

10. Convulsions or seizures

11. Eye or ear injuries or infections

12. Blows to the head that cause unconsciousness (even if brief) or have effects that last longer than fifteen minutes

13. Burns with blisters

14. Unusual rashes

15. Indications of pain (favoring a leg, wincing if a spot is touched)

16. Suspected poisoning

17. Swallowing a foreign body

## BASIC SUPPLIES

Following is a list of supplies you may want to keep on hand—but safely out of reach of your child—for first aid and routine home health care.

- Acetaminophen or ibuprofen
- Adhesive bandages (assorted sizes)
- Adhesive tape $1/2$ to 1 inch wide
- Cool mist humidifier or vaporizer
- Cotton balls
- Cotton swabs
- Diaper rash cream ointment
- Fingernail clipper
- Heating pad
- Hot water bottle
- Nasal aspirator (syringe bulb)
- Rubbing alcohol
- Sunscreen (with a label indicating an SPF of 15 or higher and no PABA)
- Syrup of ipecac
- Thermometer
- Tweezers

## FEVER GUIDE

Parents commonly think of fever as their number-one enemy when their children get sick. This leads them to battle fever aggressively with all the medication and sponge baths they can give. This is based on the mistaken notion that the fever itself is a disease and can easily harm a child.

Fever is not a disease but rather a symptom, showing that a fight against a disease or infection is going on inside the body. In that fight, excess heat is generated in the core of the body and is dissipated to the head and limbs, where it radiates off the skin. In general, pediatricians recommend not trying to lower fevers under 101°F (38.3°C) taken rectally or by ear, and they certainly don't want parents to consider fevers in and of themselves as threats to the well-being of their children. It should be said, however, that fevers in infants less than three months old are of much more concern than fevers in older infants.

Here are some facts that you should know about fevers:

## Fever levels

- The normal, average temperature measured rectally or by ear is 99.6°F (37.9°C). The normal temperature at the underarm can range from 96.6 to 97.6°F (35.9 to 36.4°C).
- A fever may be present when a rectal or ear temperature is 100°F (37.8°C) or higher.
- The height of a fever does not necessarily correlate with the severity of the disease or illness the child is fighting.
- You don't need to be checking your baby's temperature unless he feels warm or is acting sick.
- A high fever is 104°F (40.0°C) and above (by any measuring method). Harmful effects of fever itself (beyond discomfort) do not occur until the temperature reaches 106 to 107°F (41.1 to 41.7°C), and they only occur rarely. This is the highest a fever will go in humans because an automatic mechanism limits it at that point.
- There is a normal fluctuation of temperature with activity and time of day. A normal temperature is usually highest in the late afternoon and early evening.

## Fever treatment

- During your child's first three months, you should not give him any medication until you've called your doctor. Unless your physician has specifically directed you to do so, do not give your child aspirin or products that contain aspirin. Doctors have linked aspirin with Reye's syndrome, a serious condition of progressive vomiting and decreasing consciousness. Use acetaminophen or ibuprofen in liquid form to ensure more accurate doses and easier administration. Acetamino-phen also comes in rectal suppository forms to use when vomiting makes it difficult for your child to keep the medication down.
- The main reason to treat a fever is to reduce your infant's discomfort and the risk of dehydration. When fever is present, the body loses more fluid than it does under normal conditions.
- You don't need to treat a fever with medication until your baby's rectal or ear temperature goes over 101°F (38.3°C) and preferably only then if your child seems uncomfortable. Light clothing, extra fluids, and a pleasant, cool room are better treatments unless the fever is higher.
- Sponge baths and tub baths, including alcohol baths, are not recommended as routine fever treatment.

## Recommended acetaminophen and ibuprofen doses

Acetaminophen and ibuprofen come in a variety of forms and concentrations, so a dropper-full of liquid made by one manufacturer may not have the same amount of medication as another manufacturer's product. Also, some physicians refer to a baby's weight more than his age to determine how much medication to recommend. If you have questions about dosages, contact your doctor's office or a pharmacist. More guidelines for giving your baby acetaminophen and ibuprofen follow:

- Carefully measure and time the doses of acetaminophen or ibuprofen you give your child so you don't overdose him. Overdosing fever medication can result in nausea, vomiting, and excessive sweating. An overdose can be fatal. If you suspect that your child has been overdosed, call your doctor or poison-control center immediately.

- Never give more than one dose of acetaminophen in any four-hour period or ibuprofen in any six-hour period. The medication takes effect in about thirty minutes.

- Take your child's temperature before giving another dose of fever medication. He may be extremely hot; or, he may not have the fever or discomfort level he did before. Taking his temperature can track a rising fever or keep you from giving unnecessary medication.

- Don't awake your child for medication or temperature-taking. Sleep is more important than either.

## Contact the doctor's office if . . .

- your infant is less than three months old and has even a low fever. There could be a serious infection, even without other clear-cut symptoms.
- your infant is three to six months with a fever over 101°F (38.3°C).
- your child is any age with a fever over 103°F (39.4°C).

- your child has a serious underlying disease and has any degree of fever.
  *Note: If your child has experienced a seizure while having a fever, your doctor may prescribe a slightly different form of treatment when subsequent fevers occur. It's important to remember, however, that such seizures are rare, and they almost always stop by age six. (See convulsion on page 131.)*

## HOW TO TAKE TEMPERATURES

For accuracy's sake, it's preferable that infants and toddlers have their temperatures taken rectally. Note that temperatures from rectal readings will be one degree higher than others. Don't leave your child unattended while taking his temperature.

1. Shake the mercury level down to below 96°F (35.6°C).

2. Lubricate bulb with petroleum jelly.

3. Lay your child across your lap, stomach down. Gently insert the bulb and between one-half and one inch of the stem into his rectum. Keep his hand against his bottom, to prevent injury in case he wiggles. In an older infant, it may be easier to place him on the floor or changing table.

4. Take the thermometer out after the mercury has stopped rising for thirty seconds to a minute. This usually takes about two minutes.

5. Wipe off the thermometer and read the highest level of mercury; record the reading.

As an alternative to rectal readings, thermometers that can take a baby's eardrum temperature are now available.

Though expensive, these appeal to parents because they are less traumatic to the infant, quicker, and more convenient. Eardrum readings translate in the same way as rectal temperatures—one degree higher than the oral temperature. The accuracy of this method varies, especially in young infants.

Another convenient way to take a temperature is in the underarm. This method will result in a reading one to two degrees below an oral reading. It is less accurate than a rectal temperature.

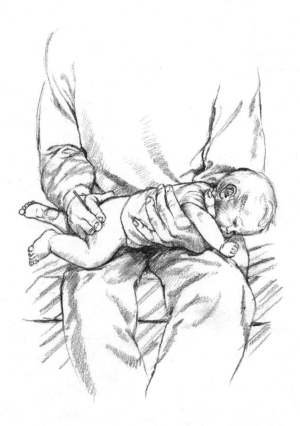

**Taking your baby's temperature**

# Symptoms Index

If you are perplexed about what illness your child may have, try looking up the symptoms you've noticed in the symptoms index. In reading them, see what other accompanying symptoms match (or don't match) your child's. Then make an educated guess about what illness your child has. Again, please don't use the guide to play doctor, and don't assume that every child with bronchiolitis, for example, will have every single symptom listed in that entry. Work closely with your doctor if you have any doubts at all.

Appetite, loss of . . . . . . . . . . . . . . . .121, 126
Bites . . . . . . . . . . . . . . . . . . . . . . . . . . . .146
Blackheads . . . . . . . . . . . . . . . . . . . . . .118
Body movement, jerking . . . . . . . . . . . . .131
Bowel movements,
        frequent . . . . . . . . . . . . . . . . . . . .138
        liquid . . . . . . . . . . . . . . . . . . . . . .138
        hard . . . . . . . . . . . . . . . . . . . . . . .130
Breathing problems . . . . . .119, 121, 124, 126,
                        135, 149, 150
Chest pain . . . . . . . . . . . . . . . . . . . . . .149
Chewing fingers or other objects . . . . . . . .153
Chills . . . . . . . . . . . . . . . . . . . . . . . . . . .140
Choking . . . . . . . . . . . . . . . . . . . .124, 150
Congestion . . . . . . . . . . . . . . . . . . . . . .140
Constipation . . . . . . . . . . . . . . . . . . . . .130
Convulsions . . . . . . . . . . . . . . . . . .131, 150
Coordination, loss of . . . . . . . . . . . . .129, 143
Cough . . . . . . . . . . . .121, 126, 132, 135, 149
Coughing blood . . . . . . . . . . . . . . . . . . .150
Crying . . . . . . . . . . . . . . . . . . . . . .127, 153
Diarrhea . . . . . . . . . . . . . . . . . . . .138, 150
Dizziness . . . . . . . . . . . . . . . .140, 143, 150
Drooling . . . . . . . . . . . . . . . . . . . .131, 153
Drowsiness . . . . . . . . . . . . . . . . . . .136, 150
Ear
        discharge from . . . . . . . . . . . . . . . .140
        sore . . . . . . . . . . . . . . . . . . . . . . .140
Eyes
        crossed . . . . . . . . . . . . . . . . . . . . .134
        discharge from . . . . . . . . . . . . . . . .148
        red . . . . . . . . . . . . . . . . . . . . . . . .148
        sunken . . . . . . . . . . . . . . . . . . . . .136
        swollen . . . . . . . . . . . . . . . . . . . . .148
        watery . . . . . . . . . . . . . . . . . . . . .126
Fever            121, 126, 135, 136, 140,
                147, 149, 151, 153
Headache . . . . . . . . . . . . . . . . . . . .129, 140

Hearing loss . . . . . . . . . . . . . . . . . . .140, 143
Heart failure . . . . . . . . . . . . . . . . . . . . . .122
Heart palpitations . . . . . . . . . . . . . . . . . .131
Hoarseness . . . . . . . . . . . . . . . . . . . . . .126
Irritability . . . . . . . . . . . . . . . . . . . .140, 153
Itching . . . . . . . . . . . . . . . . . . . . . . . . .130
Lethargic behavior . . . . . . . . . . . . . . . . . .147
Mouth, dry . . . . . . . . . . . . . . . . . . . . . .136
Muscle spasms . . . . . . . . . . . . . . . . . . . .131
Nausea . . . . . . . . . . . . . . . . . . . . .150, 153
Neck, stiffness in . . . . . . . . . . . . . .131, 147
Pimples . . . . . . . . . . . . . . . . . . . . .118, 137
Rash            133, 137, 141, 142, 144,
                145, 150, 151
Runny nose . . . . . . . . . . . . . . . . . . .126, 140
Seizures . . . . . . . . . . . . . . . . . . . . . . . .131
Skin
        bluish . . . . . . . . . . . . . . . . . . . . . .131
        discoloration         133, 137, 141, 142,
                        144, 145, 146
        dry . . . . . . . . . . . . . . . . . . . . .136, 141
        scaling of . . . . . . . . . . . . . .133, 141, 145
Sleeplessness . . . . . . . . . . . . . . . . . . . . .140
Sneezing . . . . . . . . . . . . . . . . . . . . . . . .126
Speech development, slow . . . . . . . . . . . . .143
Stomach pain . . . . . . . . . . . . . . . . .149, 151
Unconsciousness . . . . . . . . . . . .129, 131, 150
Urinary discharge . . . . . . . . . . . . . . . . . .153
Urine
        bloody . . . . . . . . . . . . . . . . . . . . . .153
        foul smelling . . . . . . . . . . . . . . . . . .153
        frequent . . . . . . . . . . . . . . . . . . . .153
        infrequent . . . . . . . . . . . . . . . . . . .136
        painful . . . . . . . . . . . . . . . . . . . . . .153
Vomiting . . . . . . . . . .129, 131, 147, 151, 156
Whiteheads . . . . . . . . . . . . . . . . . . . . . .118
White patches on tongue
        and/or inside the mouth . . . . . . . . . .152

# Acne (Newborn)

## DESCRIPTION

A common condition in newborns that causes the skin to break out in pimples.

## WHAT YOU NEED TO KNOW

- Newborn acne is common and cures itself. It often appears at three to six weeks of age and disappears or improves significantly on its own over time. The time span may be days or months.
- Pimples are most often found in oily areas of the skin, such as around the nose, on the back, or near the scalp

## SUPPLIES

Washcloth, soap, and water

## SYMPTOMS

- Blackheads (pimples with dark centers)
- Whiteheads (pimples with white centers)

## GET PROFESSIONAL HELP IF

Your infant's skin seems to be looking especially dry, irritated, weepy, or possibly infected.

## WHAT TO CHECK

Does your baby's acne seem to be spreading rapidly and causing discomfort?

## TREATMENT

Wash your newborn's acne gently with a wet washcloth, then dry the area. The clogged pores should open and heal by themselves without further treatment.

# Breathing Emergency

## DESCRIPTION

A life-threatening situation resulting from a blocked airway, electric shock, or other condition.

## WHAT YOU NEED TO KNOW

- Time is critical. Act quickly while someone calls for emergency help.
- A CPR course prepares you for this emergency. Use the techniques on the following page only if you are trained in CPR. Administering CPR without adequate training is dangerous.
- If choking is the cause, follow the procedures on page 124 to dislodge the object, then begin emergency breathing if needed, as described below.
- If electric shock is the cause, do not touch the child directly if he is still touching the source of the electricity. Turn off the electric current, remove the fuse (or trip the circuit breaker), or stand on a nonconducting mat, such as a rubber door mat, and push the child away from the source of the current with a nonconducting object like a dry board or rope. Never use a wet or metal object.
- Don't tilt the child's head if you suspect a back or neck injury.

## SUPPLIES

None

## GET PROFESSIONAL HELP IF

A child's breathing stops. Follow the procedures on the following page until emergency help arrives.

# Breathing Emergency
# Step-by-Step

**1** GENTLY SHAKE the baby to see if he is unconscious. If conscious, he will respond and breathe. If unconscious, check for breathing. Tilt the head back and place your ear close to his mouth. Look, listen, and feel for breathing.

**2** IF HE IS NOT BREATHING, turn the infant on his back on a firm surface. If you do not suspect choking, cover his mouth and nostrils with your mouth and give two slow breaths or pinch the nose closed with one hand and breathe into the mouth (1 to 1¹/₂ seconds per breath). Then pause to take a breath and repeat.

**3** CHECK FOR BREATHING. If you do not see the chest rise and fall when you give breaths, readjust the head tilt and try again. If that does not work, follow the procedures for choking on page 124, and then begin mouth-to-mouth breathing. If the baby has no pulse, see page 123 for CPR instructions. Otherwise, continue breathing for the baby until help arrives.

# Bronchiolitis

## DESCRIPTION

Inflammation and constriction, or narrowing, of the smallest air passages (bronchioles) due to viral infection, most often a respiratory syncytial virus (RSV).

## WHAT YOU NEED TO KNOW

- Bronchiolitis occurs mostly in infants. Bronchitis, which is the infection of larger airways, is rare in infants.
- Bronchiolitis has many of the same symptoms as pneumonia.
- It usually lasts several days or even weeks, but will resolve by itself.
- RSV infections are more common in the winter months.
- Ear infections can accompany bronchiolitis.
- Some children develop asthma following bronchiolitis.

## SUPPLIES

Thermometer, prescribed medication, clear liquids, cool-mist humidifier or nebulizers

## SYMPTOMS

- Runny nose
- Rapid, shallow breathing
- Labored breathing:
  —Nostrils widen and move more often
  —Muscles between the ribs move in and out due to increased work with breathing
  —Grunting sounds
  —Wheezing (a high-pitched noise, especially when exhaling)
- Fever*
- Cough
- Loss of appetite

## GET PROFESSIONAL HELP IF

- The above symptoms are present, especially if breathing is labored.
- Your baby's lips or skin appear blue, or he seems to be tiring from the increased effort to breathe.
- Your infant refuses fluids or several feedings for a day or vomits what he drinks.
- There is an underlying medical condition, such as heart disease or prematurity, along with bronchiolitis symptoms.

## WHAT TO CHECK

- Note temperature daily.
- Monitor symptoms.

## TREATMENT

Follow the treatment recommended by your doctor. It may include these elements:

- Prescribed oral medication
- Frequent clear liquids, breast milk, or formula
- Humidifying the air
- Nebulizer treatments, which are a way to give medication in mist form, by a special machine
- Using a nasal aspirator with salt and water drops

* See fever guide, pages 113–116.

# Cardiac Arrest

## DESCRIPTION

A life-threatening condition when the heart stops due to breathing emergency or other situation.

## WHAT YOU NEED TO KNOW

- A CPR course prepares you for this emergency.

- Use the techniques on the following page only if you are trained in CPR. Administering CPR without adequate training is dangerous.

- If choking may be the cause, follow the procedure on page 124.

## SUPPLIES

None

## GET PROFESSIONAL HELP IF

An infant's heartbeat or breathing stops. Follow the steps below while waiting for emergency help.

# Cardiac Arrest
# Step-by-Step

### Treatment—BREATHING

See page 120 for emergency breathing instructions. Return to this page for circulation treatment.

### Treatment—CIRCULATION

**1** TO CHECK the pulse, place the tips of two fingers on the artery inside the infant's elbow. Do not press hard. If there is no pulse, begin chest compressions.

**2** FOR INFANTS, push on the middle of the sternum (breastbone) between the nipples with two or three fingers. Compress the sternum ½ to 1 inch about 100 times per minute (twice a second). Don't apply too much pressure.

**3** CONTINUE breathing for the baby as you compress the chest. After every fifth compression give one puff. Support the baby's back with one hand to help keep the head tilted and keep your face close to the baby's to make it easier to breathe and continue chest compressions.

**4** GET EMERGENCY help after breathing is established if you are alone, or send someone for help while you continue CPR.

# Choking

## DESCRIPTION

A life-threatening obstruction of the airway by an object, food, or croup.

## WHAT YOU NEED TO KNOW

- The signals of choking include bluish lips, nails, and skin; the inability to vocalize, breathe, or cry; high-pitched noises and ineffective coughs.
- Do not interfere with your infant or call for help if he can still vocalize, cough, or breathe. Let your baby cough and don't try to remove the object, as this may push it further down.
- If breathing has stopped and the baby is unconscious, call for emergency help, then attempt to restore breathing. Start giving breaths as indicated on page 120 and use choking procedures if the airway is blocked.

## SUPPLIES

None

## GET PROFESSIONAL HELP IF

Choking results in your baby not being able to talk or make noise, and he turns blue. Have someone call the rescue squad while you begin emergency procedures.

# Choking
# Step-by-Step

**TREATMENT**

Note: These instructions pertain to infants less than one year old. Techniques for older children are different.

**1** STRADDLE the infant over your arm, keeping the head lower than the trunk, face down with his upper chest and jaw in your hand. Rest your forearm against your body to provide further support. Give four quick blows between his shoulder blades with the heel of your hand.

**2** IF HE still cannot breathe, quickly turn him up on your other arm, resting your arm on your leg. Give four quick chest thrusts on the sternum (between the nipples) with two fingers.

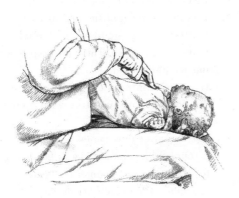

**3** PLACE your thumb in the mouth on the tongue and put your fingers around the chin. Lift the jaw and look in the mouth for the foreign object. If you see the object, remove it with your finger. Do not attempt a finger sweep of the mouth unless you can see the object.

**4** IF THE baby is unconscious, follow the sequence of breaths, blows, thrusts, looks. Whether or not you dislodge the object, start with the emergency breathing steps on page 120 and then repeat the sequence on this page. If the baby begins to breathe, stop giving breaths.

# Cold

## DESCRIPTION

A common, contagious viral infection of the nasal and throat membranes, frequently involving the ears and chest.

## WHAT YOU NEED TO KNOW

- Newborns and young infants will often sneeze and bring up mucus that is residual from birth. These are not the signs of a cold.
- Most infants have eight to ten colds in their first two years of life.
- Colds are most contagious in the first three to four days; symptoms usually subside after the third day without treatment. Colds spread most commonly through coughing and sneezing, but also from the hands.
- Antibiotics don't cure colds and may worsen them or upset an infant's stomach.
- Ear infections are the most common complication.

## SUPPLIES

Thermometer, liquids, nasal aspirator, acetaminophen or ibuprofen, saline drops (consisting of half a teaspoon salt and one cup water or available commercially)

## SYMPTOMS

- Congested, runny nose, with thin and clear mucus early on but often thick and colored as the cold progresses
- Red, watery eyes
- Sneezing
- Cough/hoarseness
- Breathing difficulty
- Listlessness or irritability
- Decreased appetite
- Fever*
- Sore throat or difficulty swallowing
- Mild swelling of the lymph nodes

## GET PROFESSIONAL HELP IF

- Mucus becomes thick and colored.
- Your baby is less than six months old and has cold symptoms.
- A cough persists for more than a week.
- Breathing seems labored.
- Lips or fingernails take on a blue color.
- Your infant becomes particularly irritable or listless.
- It seems that your baby is experiencing pain in one or both ears.
- There is a fever above 101°F.

## WHAT TO CHECK

Check temperature if your infant seems warm or sick.

## TREATMENT

- Offer water or juice every hour. With infants less than six months old, clear mucus from the nose with a nasal aspirator before feedings and naps. If this procedure seems to be causing discomfort or irritation, try using normal saline drops.
- Place infant on his side for sleeping.
- Elevate the head of the bed using the mattress rungs or by putting books under the mattress. This may help the mucus drain better.
- Give acetaminophen or ibuprofen for fever after consulting with your physician.
- Use only over-the-counter medications if your health care provider directs you to do so. Over-the-counter medications can make the secretions thicker and have other side effects.
- A cool-mist humidifier may help thin the mucus. Make sure you follow cleaning instructions.

*See fever guide, pages 113–116.*

# Colic

## DESCRIPTION

Prolonged periods of intense crying in infants, occurring on a daily basis. Though there is no full medical explanation, it could be related to intestinal contractions and digestive pain.

## WHAT YOU NEED TO KNOW

- Colic occurs in one in five babies between two weeks and three months of age.
- Colic can be quite frustrating to parents, because there seems to be no reason for the crying, yet it may continue for hours.
- Evidence suggests that some cases of colic are related to a nursing mother's intake of cows' milk or other potentially irritating foods.
- Colicky babies fed cows' milk-based formula may benefit from changing to another formula type.
- Almost all babies have a regular fussy period in the evening, but this is not defined as colic.

## SUPPLIES

Thermometer, pacifier, hot water bottle or heating pad

## SYMPTOMS

- Crying that persists around the clock
- Acting hungry, but then crying partway through feeding
- Drawing up legs to body; clenching fists
- Enlarged stomach from gas on a regular basis

## GET PROFESSIONAL HELP IF

- You suspect colic but want to be reassured no other medical problem exists.
- Your baby cries persistently for more than four hours.
- There is a fever,* runny nose, cough, vomiting, or other signs of illness.
- Colic does not subside by age four months.
- You need peer support to pull you through this challenging time.

## WHAT TO CHECK

- Possible causes of discomfort, such as illness, diaper rash, or hard, pellet-like stools.
- If bottlefeeding, ensure proper formula preparation and feeding. Make sure the formula flows from the upended bottle at one drop per second.

## TREATMENT

- Test out a variety of methods to soothe your baby; there is no sure-fire treatment, and it is possible no method will have results. Be patient and wait it out. Try these methods:
  —cuddling, swaddling (see pages 20–22), rocking, walking
  —a trip in a car or a baby carrier
  —using a pacifier or "white noise," such as a vacuum cleaner, hair dryer, washing machine, or clothes dryer
  —placing your baby on his stomach across your knees, and rubbing his back
  —burping your baby frequently
  —applying mild heat to the abdomen
- Don't overstimulate your baby by too much jiggling or movement
- For mothers nursing their children, eliminate cows' milk from your diet for two weeks to see if it has an effect.
- Remember that colic is temporary and will disappear with time.

*See fever guide, pages 113–116.

- Get some rest from caring for your infant, even if only for a few hours. You may feel reluctant to leave your colicky infant with another provider, but it is critical that you get a break if you are feeling tense.
- Discuss your frustration with others.

# Concussion/Head Injury

## DESCRIPTION

A brief, temporary loss of consciousness following a hard knock or blow to the head.

## WHAT YOU NEED TO KNOW

- Minor head injuries are common and inevitable but are rarely a cause for concern.
- Serious injuries can cause internal bleeding that puts pressure on the brain. Symptoms can appear even one to two days following the injury.
- Even with a loss of consciousness, though there is a brief disturbance in the brain, most often there will be no serious consequences or damage.
- A good rule: The infant is well if he acts well.

## SUPPLIES

Ice

## SYMPTOMS

Note: These symptoms will vary according to the severity and location of the injury.
- Some scalp bleeding, a "goose egg," crying up to ten minutes—common after a minor bump
- Odd behavior or loss of alertness— signs of a more serious injury
- Vomiting

## GET PROFESSIONAL HELP IF

- Baby loses consciousness.
- Infant vomits more than twice.
- One pupil becomes larger than the other.
- Baby behaves abnormally, experiences a loss of coordination, shows any seizure activity, or is persistently irritable.
- Baby suffers a cut that is deep or bleeds significantly (it might need stitches).

## WHAT TO CHECK

- How does your baby act? If the injury is serious, it most likely will result in abnormal behavior.
- Watch baby closely for twenty-four to forty-eight hours after the injury. If the blow is hard, you may be advised to wake the infant a few times for night checks.

## TREATMENT

- Watch the infant for abnormal behavior.
- Apply ice to the injured area to relieve pain and reduce swelling.
- Treat blows that cause bleeding and swelling with ice and pressure. Head cuts bleed easily. Wash them with soap and water.

# Constipation

## DESCRIPTION

Hard bowel movements.

## WHAT YOU NEED TO KNOW

- Constipation is often overdiagnosed. It may be related to diet or illness, or more rarely to a congenital defect of the large intestine. Breast-fed babies rarely get constipation.
- Infants differ greatly in their bowel habits; constipation refers to stool consistency only, not frequency. After one to two months, breast-fed babies may have very infrequent bowel movements.
- When you start your baby on solid foods, the stools will often change. Rice cereal and bananas tend to have a slight constipating effect, so you should balance them with less constipating solids.

## SUPPLIES

Fruit juice, extra water

## SYMPTOMS

- Hard stools
- Painful bowel movements

## GET PROFESSIONAL HELP IF

- Movements seem painful, with pain subsiding afterward.
- Stools are bloody.
- Stools are pelletlike, firm, and dry.
- Constipation recurs frequently.
- The condition does not improve with home treatment.

## WHAT TO CHECK

Is your child drinking less fluid than usual or eating more solid foods that cause constipation?

## TREATMENT

- Try giving your baby small amounts (one to two teaspoons) of prune juice. Use one part water to one part prune juice. Trial and error is the best way to determine your baby's ideal amount.
- Consider increasing high-fiber solids, such as peas, beans, broccoli, apricots, plums, and prunes.
- Increase your baby's water intake.
- Consult your physician by phone before giving such home remedies as laxatives, enemas, suppositories, or mineral oil. Do not attempt to stimulate a bowel movement with a rectal thermometer unless your doctor has instructed you to do so.

# Convulsion (Fit, Seizure)

## DESCRIPTION

A series of involuntary muscle spasms, in which the body often stiffens. Caused by abnormal electrical impulses in the brain, they are sometimes associated with periods of temporary unconsciousness or confusion. In infants, seizures may manifest themselves in more subtle ways.

## WHAT YOU NEED TO KNOW

- A seizure is usually not life-threatening. Most seizures result from fever (especially up to age three and rarely after age six). Fever-related seizures usually end within five minutes and have no lasting effects.
- Most seizures will stop on their own.
- Other less common causes include poisoning, severe infection, and epilepsy.

## SUPPLIES

Thermometer, cool water and washcloth, acetaminophen suppository

## SYMPTOMS

- Blue face and lips
- Uncontrolled, jerking body movements; rigidity or stiffness
- Vomiting/drooling
- Rolling eyes

## GET PROFESSIONAL HELP IF

- It is your child's first seizure. It's okay to call for emergency medical assistance for any seizure, though it usually will have stopped by the time help arrives.
- A seizure lasts more than two or three minutes or is especially severe.

## WHAT TO CHECK

- How does your infant act before and after convulsions?
- How long did the seizure last?
- Did it affect one or both sides of the body?
- Is there a fever,* or are symptoms of infection or poisoning (see page 150) present?

## TREATMENT

- Remove surrounding objects the infant may injure himself on.
- Turn infant on side to prevent choking on vomit or saliva.
- Loosen tight clothing.
- Don't place anything in his mouth, such as tongue depressors, fingers, liquids, or medication, while the seizure is in progress.
- Once the seizure is over, treat any fever as you normally would, or give an acetaminophen suppository.
- Get medical assistance.

*\* See fever guide, pages 113–116.*

# Cough

## DESCRIPTION

A reflexive spasm in response to an irritation or infection of the respiratory system.

## WHAT YOU NEED TO KNOW

- Coughing can be caused by a variety of conditions, including virus, bacterial infection, asthma, allergy, or respiratory blockage.
- Coughing helps clear the respiratory system of irritants and foreign objects.

## SUPPLIES

Thermometer; liquids, such as water and fruit juices; cool-mist humidifier (optional); nonprescription cough medicine (optional)

## SYMPTOMS

Coughing itself is a symptom of some other conditions. (See the symptoms index on page 117 for cross references.)

## GET PROFESSIONAL HELP IF

- Your child is less than two months old and has a persistent cough.
- Breathing is rapid, difficult, or wheezy.
- Fever* is persistent.
- A cough lasts more than one week.
- A foreign object has been swallowed.

## WHAT TO CHECK

- Try to identify the cause of the cough to decide what treatment to use.
- Check your infant's temperature every four to six hours if he seems warm.
- Note whether the cough is worse during the day, night, or both.

## TREATMENT

- Treatment will depend on the type of cough.
- Give plenty of liquids to soothe the throat and loosen the mucus.
- Cool-mist humidifiers may soothe irritation with croup and bronchiolitis, but it is important that you clean them daily.
- In general, use medicine only if coughing is interfering with sleep or making your baby tired. Consult your physician about what medication you should give. Expectorants, decongestants, antihistamines, and suppressants all have different uses and possible side effects.
- Elevating the head of the crib may help.

*See fever guide, pages 113–116.

# Cradle Cap/Seborrhea

## DESCRIPTION

A skin and/or scalp condition characterized by oily, yellowish scales or crusted patches.

## WHAT YOU NEED TO KNOW

- Cradle cap is most common in infants but occurs in children as old as age six.
- It usually appears on the scalp but may appear as scaliness or redness on the forehead, the eyebrows, behind the ears, or in the groin area, where there is a concentration of oil-producing glands.
- It can be a recurring condition, but will often improve by itself during the first month.

## SUPPLIES

Washcloth, soap and water, fine-tooth comb, baby oil, towel

## SYMPTOMS

- Yellowish scales
- Crusty patches of skin with slight redness in surrounding areas

## GET PROFESSIONAL HELP IF

The condition persists after several weeks of home treatment.

## WHAT TO CHECK

Watch for signs of skin infection. Children with cradle cap are susceptible.

## TREATMENT

- Wash the affected area daily with soap and water, using a washcloth. For the scalp, shampoo the hair frequently, daily if necessary.
- Remove scales with a fine-tooth comb or brush.
- For severe cases, try rubbing a little baby oil into the affected area and cover it with a warm towel for fifteen minutes. Then shampoo, work scales loose with a comb, and wash away.
- A medicated shampoo that helps dissolve the scales or a cortisone cream or lotion may be the solution in more stubborn cases. Consult your health care provider before using these.

# Crossed Eyes

## DESCRIPTION

Inward or outward turning of one or both eyes rather than parallel eye motion or position.

## WHAT YOU NEED TO KNOW

- Periodic crossing of the eyes is normal in newborns and should be markedly improved by two to three months.
- Premature infants are at a higher risk for this condition.

## SUPPLIES

None

## SYMPTOMS

- One or both eyes appearing crossed most or all of the time beyond age two to three months
- Eyes not moving synchronously

## GET PROFESSIONAL HELP IF

The eyes seem crossed, appear to wander, or don't seem to track together after the first few months of age. If you have any doubts, see an ophthalmologist or eye specialist recommended by your health care provider. If present, the condition must be treated to prevent permanent damage.

## WHAT TO CHECK

Don't be fooled: If your baby has a flat nasal bridge and skin folds on the insides of the eyes, it may create the illusion that the eyes are crossed. Your health care provider should be able to make a better judgment.

## TREATMENT

- There are no home remedies. If you suspect crossed eyes, have your primary physician recommend an ophthalmologist to visit.
- Doctor's treatment may involve wearing a patch over one eye, prescribing glasses, or performing surgery.

# Croup

## DESCRIPTION

A barking cough or labored breathing caused by inflammation and constriction, or narrowing, of airways.

## WHAT YOU NEED TO KNOW

- An attack often comes on suddenly (usually at night), for no apparent reason. It requires immediate home treatment.
- Children under age three are most susceptible because their air passages are small.
- If it's severe and doesn't respond to home treatment, an attack may require emergency room treatment.
- Croup is almost always caused by a virus.

## SUPPLIES

Thermometer, vaporizer, acetaminophen or ibuprofen, liquids

## SYMPTOMS

- A hacking cough that sounds like the bark of a seal or dog
- Difficulty breathing air into the lungs
- Fever*

## GET PROFESSIONAL HELP IF

- Symptoms rapidly worsen and home treatment doesn't ease the condition to allow the infant to fall asleep.
- Fever is above 103°F (39.4°C).
- Your baby turns blue, drools, or appears to be struggling to breathe.
- Your infant can't vocalize.

## WHAT TO CHECK

Don't leave your infant unattended during an attack. Because an attack may occur several nights in a row, watch him closely for three nights.

## TREATMENT

- Though most cases can be treated at home, contact your doctor at the onset of an attack.
- Take your child into the bathroom, close the door, and run hot water to generate steam.
- As an alternative to steam or if steam doesn't help, take the baby into the cool, outside air for twenty minutes. If there is still no improvement, seek help immediately.
- If the doctor determines home treatment is sufficient, put a cool-mist humidifier or vaporizer in the room, and give acetaminophen and liquids.
- Don't give cough syrup.

*See fever guide, pages 113–116.*

# Dehydration

## DESCRIPTION

A condition in which there is an insufficient amount of fluid in the body.

## WHAT YOU NEED TO KNOW

- The most common causes are diarrhea and vomiting.
- Other causes are excessive sweating and urination. With a fever, the body loses extra fluid through the skin.
- Body fluids contain important salts and minerals that must be replaced when the child is dehydrated.

## SUPPLIES

Thermometer; clear liquids, specifically oral rehydration solutions or commercial electrolyte mixes such as Lytren, Pedialyte, Infalyte, or Ricelyte

## SYMPTOMS

- Dry mouth
- Sunken eyes and fontanel (soft spot on the head)
- Drowsiness
- Lack of energy
- Either dry or doughy-textured skin
- Decreased urine output
- Decreased or absent tears when crying
- Fever*

## GET PROFESSIONAL HELP IF

- Symptoms are severe and the infant is generally either excessively sleepy or fussy.
- Your infant is not able to keep down liquids due to persistent vomiting or diarrhea.
- Home remedies don't improve the condition.
- Your child has diabetes and shows signs of dehydration.

## WHAT TO CHECK

Is your infant urinating infrequently (fewer than six wet diapers per day)? If so, increase liquid consumption.

## TREATMENT

Frequently give small amounts of cool liquids—preferably a commercially prepared electrolyte mix—if the cause is vomiting. But allow a short rest period after the last spell of vomiting. The recommended amount of liquids or electrolyte mix for infants during a six-hour period is at least six ounces.

*See fever guide, pages 113–116.*

# Diaper Rash

## DESCRIPTION

A rash on a baby's bottom in the areas covered by a diaper.

## WHAT YOU NEED TO KNOW

- Diapers with urine or stool in them cause the rashes. One simple cure is letting your baby go bare-bottomed to allow air on the skin.
- Yeast is a common cause of persistent diaper rash and requires specific medication for treatment. If your baby is taking an antibiotic, there is an increased chance of yeast infection.
- Plastic pants or tight gathers in disposable diapers can aggravate the rash.
- Most babies get some form of diaper rash at one time or another.

## SUPPLIES

Water, a doctor-recommended diaper rash ointment

## SYMPTOMS

Red patches, with or without tiny pimples, on skin areas covered by the diaper

## GET PROFESSIONAL HELP IF

- The rash starts looking angry or rash pimples develop whiteheads or blisters.
- Home treatment fails to improve the rash in a few days.

## WHAT TO CHECK

Is the baby allergic to some substance that comes in contact with the red area? Possibilities include plastic pants, disposable diapers, detergents, powders, lanolin, perfumes, alcohol, lotions, and fabric softeners.

## TREATMENT

- Increase the frequency of diaper changes, and clean your baby carefully each time with plain water. Let all the water dry before putting on a new diaper.
- Apply zinc oxide ointment or a topical barrier ointment between skin and diaper.
- Let the baby go diaperless as much as possible.
- If yeast infection is the cause, you should get a recommendation from your health care provider on what type of medication to use.

# Diarrhea

## DESCRIPTION

Frequent loose, watery bowel movements that are yellowish, light brown, or green.

## WHAT YOU NEED TO KNOW

- Causes include viruses, bacteria, parasites, diet change, antibiotics, or intolerance to milk.
- Breast-fed infants will have up to twelve loose bowel movements a day in the first few months. This is a normal pattern, not diarrhea.
- Often diarrhea is present with colds, sore throat, or infections of the stomach and intestines.
- Diarrhea, when accompanied by vomiting, can lead to dehydration.

## SUPPLIES

Thermometer; commercial electrolyte mixes such as Lytren, Pedialyte, Ricelyte, and Infalyte

## SYMPTOMS

- Liquid bowel movements
- Bowel movements increasing in frequency to more than two a day

## GET PROFESSIONAL HELP IF

- Loose bowel movements occur more than once every hour or two for more than twelve hours.
- A fever of 102.5°F (39.1°C) or higher persists for more than one to two days.*
- Blood is present in stools.
- There are signs of dehydration.
- Your baby seems to be in pain.
- Diarrhea persists for more than two weeks, even if mild.
- Your infant refuses to eat or drink anything.

## WHAT TO CHECK

- Are there signs of dehydration? (See page 136.)
- Is your infant passing urine normally?
- How frequent are your infant's bowel movements and what is their consistency?
- Has your infant's diet changed recently?
- Check his temperature if he feels warm.

## TREATMENT

- If the diarrhea is mild (fewer than six to eight watery stools a day), you can usually keep your infant on his normal diet.
- For more severe diarrhea, rest the intestinal tract by stopping breast milk or formula and solid foods for no more than twenty-four hours.
- During this time, frequently provide clear liquids, in small amounts, to satisfy thirst and prevent dehydration. There is no need to push clear liquids; you merely need to make them available. Do not keep your baby on clear liquids alone any longer than necessary, certainly not longer than twenty-four hours. The ideal solution is to offer your baby commercially prepared rehydration liquids. Do not use heavily sugared beverages, and never use boiled skim milk.
- After twenty-four hours off food, if your infant is eating solids, begin feeding him rice, applesauce, pears, bananas, crackers, toast, or cereal.
- On the third day, return to the normal diet.

*See fever guide, pages 113–116.*

- Put petroleum jelly, zinc oxide, or other topical barrier on the buttocks or around the diaper area if it is sore.

- Do not use over-the-counter antidiarrheal medications. They can actually worsen the condition.

# Ear Infection

## DESCRIPTION

An inflammation or accumulation of fluid in the middle ear, usually caused by bacterial infection.

## WHAT YOU NEED TO KNOW

- Two out of three children experience at least one ear infection by age two.
- Colds often cause the Eustachian tubes to swell and close, especially in infants. Fluids build up in the middle ear, causing pain and sometimes temporary hearing loss.
- Ear infections occur more often in the winter and early spring.
- A baby who takes a bottle while lying flat may increase the chance of developing an infection.

## SUPPLIES

Thermometer, acetaminophen or ibuprofen, prescribed eardrops, heating pad or hot water bottle

## SYMPTOMS

- Chills and fever*
- Congestion, runny nose, especially with yellow or green drainage
- Ear discharge
- Fussiness
- Inability to sleep
- Apparent hearing loss
- Rubbing/tugging at ear
- Crying during feeding
- Eye mattering or discharge

## GET PROFESSIONAL HELP IF

- Your infant tugs or rubs his ear(s).
- Balance problems or apparent loss of hearing develops.
- Your baby's temperature is over 101°F (38.3°C).
- The eardrum ruptures. Look for yellow to red fluid or pus draining from the ear.

## WHAT TO CHECK

Monitor fever.

## TREATMENT

- Apply heating pad or hot water bottle to the ear.
- See a physician, even if treatment relieves the pain. Antibiotics may be necessary to clear the infection. Make sure you follow through with treatment and medication, even after symptoms seem to subside.
- Give acetaminophen or ibuprofen, after consulting with your physician.
- You may want to use doctor-recommended eardrops to treat pain or discharge. Warm the bottle; lay the infant on his back with his head turned to his side; pull out, down, and back on the earlobe. Trickle eardrops into the ear hole so that they can run all the way in.
- Follow up the ear infection with your doctor because complications can occur.

*See fever guide, pages 113–116.*

# Eczema

## DESCRIPTION

A condition characterized by a dry, scaly skin rash and intense itching. Often inherited, the skin can be bumpy and moist at times.

## WHAT YOU NEED TO KNOW

- The cause is unknown. Outbreaks may be triggered by too-frequent bathing, an allergic reaction, or dry winter heat.
- Children with eczema are at increased risk to develop food sensitivities, asthma, and allergies later in life.
- Eczema often disappears with the use of the proper lotions.
- Infant eczema usually occurs on the face, in the bends of the elbows, and behind the knees.
- Touching an irritant or allergen can cause a type of eczema at the site of contact.

## SUPPLIES

Moisturizers, nonprescription or prescription hydrocortisone ointment, super-fatted soap (Basis, Lowila, Aveeno, Oilatum), vaporizer or humidifier, nail clipper

## SYMPTOMS

- Pink or red rash
- Intense itching
- When scratched, rash oozes a moist substance that dries and aggravates itching

## GET PROFESSIONAL HELP IF

- Home treatment does not improve the condition within a week.
- The rash appears infected.

## WHAT TO CHECK

- Was a new food, clothing, or substance recently introduced to your infant's skin or environment?
- Is soap rinsed thoroughly from your baby's body after baths?
- Do other relatives have eczema?

## TREATMENT

- Use moisturizers regularly.
- Relieve itching with a doctor-recommended hydrocortisone ointment.
- Use super-fatted soap and give baths less frequently and for shorter periods of time.
- Cut your infant's fingernails short (see page 35) to reduce irritation from scratching. Keep air moist with a vaporizer or cool-mist humidifier.
- If a particular food is the cause, eliminate it from your infant's diet. However, do not attempt extensive dietary changes without a doctor's supervision.
- Avoid wool or irritating clothing.
- Oral anti-itching medications may be prescribed in severe cases.

# Fifth Disease

## DESCRIPTION

A harmless but contagious rash that disappears on its own and is caused by a virus called parvovirus.

## WHAT YOU NEED TO KNOW

- The rash usually first appears on the face, looking as if the baby's cheeks have been slapped. A lace-like rash may also appear on the trunk.
- It can take up to two weeks for symptoms to appear after the baby is infected.
- It is common, harmless, and self-curing.

## SUPPLIES

Thermometer

## SYMPTOMS

- Red, lacy rash that begins on the face and spreads to the back of arms and legs
- Fading and intensifying of rash from hour to hour for about ten days
- Presence of cold symptoms

## GET PROFESSIONAL HELP IF

- Your baby has a rash, and you believe something more serious has caused it.
- You are a pregnant mother who has been exposed to it.

## WHAT TO CHECK

Is there a fever* or any other symptom? If so, the rash is probably not fifth disease.

## TREATMENT

- There is no treatment and no need for treatment.
- It may recur for weeks, especially in response to skin irritation and temperature extremes. Still, no treatment is required.

*See fever guide, pages 113–116.

# Hearing Loss

## DESCRIPTION

Partial or total loss of hearing resulting from a congenital defect, illness, or injury.

## WHAT YOU NEED TO KNOW

- Sudden loss of hearing is usually temporary and probably indicates blockage of the eardrum by a foreign object, infection, or wax.
- A history of deafness in your family should increase your suspicions of hearing loss in your child.

## SUPPLIES

Thermometer, prescribed medication

## SYMPTOMS

- Lack of response to sounds
- Slow or absent speech development
- Difficulty with balance, coordination

## GET PROFESSIONAL HELP IF

- Your baby does not startle or turn in response to sound by age three to four months and doesn't seem to notice you until he sees you.
- The child does not begin to use a few words by age one.
- At any time you have reason to suspect that your child is not hearing well.

## WHAT TO CHECK

- Have you observed the startle reflex in your newborn? (See page 16.)
- Try a squeak toy at a quiet time to see if your baby reacts to the sound.
- Have your health care provider set up a formal hearing test by an audiologist if you have any doubts.

## TREATMENT

- A doctor should treat all conditions that cause an ear infection or other suspected cause of hearing loss.
- Do not attempt to remove a foreign object from the ear; see your health care provider.
- Do not insert any object—even a cotton swab—into the ear to remove wax. Let your doctor remove the wax at your child's next checkup.

# Heat Rash (Prickly Heat)/Heat Stroke

## DESCRIPTION

Small red bumps in skin folds, especially likely to occur on the neck and upper chest of a newborn. Heat stroke occurs when a baby is in a hot place, such as a beach or a closed car; it results in a fever.

## WHAT YOU NEED TO KNOW

- Heat rash is very common and causes only minor discomfort.
- Heat rash is caused by the blockage of pores leading to sweat glands.
- Never leave a baby in a closed car on a summer day.
- When going out in the sun, dress your child in lightweight cotton with long sleeves and a hat to prevent sunburn.

## SUPPLIES

Equipment needed for cool baths

## SYMPTOMS

Many tiny bumps in folds of skin, most often seen on cheeks, neck, shoulders, creases in skin, and diaper area

## GET PROFESSIONAL HELP IF

- Blisters appear on the bumps.
- A fever develops after a baby gets overheated.
- Your baby has a sunburn that blisters.

## WHAT TO CHECK

- Is laundry thoroughly rinsed? Some detergents and bleaches aggravate heat rash.
- Is the baby overdressed? It may contribute to heat rash.
- Are oily skin products blocking pores?

## TREATMENT

- Keep baby's skin as cool and dry as possible.
- Give frequent, cool baths or sponging to help open skin pores. Fanning may help as well. This treatment is also effective for sunburn.
- Dress the infant as lightly as possible in natural fibers. Put the baby in an air-conditioned environment if possible.

# Impetigo

## DESCRIPTION

A contagious bacterial infection of the skin, often around the nose, mouth, and ears.

## WHAT YOU NEED TO KNOW

- Impetigo can spread rapidly from one part of the body to another or from child to child through contact.
- Though not serious, it must be treated with care and persistence.

## SUPPLIES

Soap and water, compresses, prescription or nonprescription antibiotic ointment, nail clipper

## SYMPTOMS

- Yellowish bumps or scabs on the surface of the skin, often occurring in groups, with or without a honey-colored oozing fluid or crust
- Possible blisters

## GET PROFESSIONAL HELP IF

- Impetigo seems to be spreading or not responding to home treatment after five days.
- Your infant's urine turns red or cola-colored—a symptom of a rare kidney complication of impetigo.

## WHAT TO CHECK

- Because impetigo is contagious, check other family members for signs of infection.
- Make sure each family member uses his or her own towel and washcloth.

## TREATMENT

- Clean the skin with soap and water, then soak sores with a compress for ten minutes.
- Rub away the crust and pus when the crust softens.
- Cover sores with antibiotic cream three times a day. Continue treatment three to four times a day until all sores lose their scabs.
- Clip your infant's nails (see page 35) to discourage scratching, which spreads the disease.

# Insect, Animal, or Human Bites

## DESCRIPTION

An impression or break in the skin resulting from a bite or sting.

## WHAT YOU NEED TO KNOW

- Most animal bites come from familiar creatures, such as neighborhood pets.
- Human bites pose a higher risk of infection than animal bites.
- Stitches increase the chances of infection, though they are sometimes necessary for deep wounds.
- Insect bites usually cause only mild, local reactions. However, in rare cases, they can result in a more severe allergic reaction.
- Insect repellents should contain no more than 10 percent DEET (diethyltoluamide). DEET is the active ingredient, but high levels can be harmful.
- Scented soaps attract insects.

## SUPPLIES

Soap and water, washcloth, a bee-sting kit for allergic infants, calamine lotion, fingernail clipper

## SYMPTOMS

Signs of an infected wound include the following:
- Pus or drainage
- Swelling, tenderness, and warmth around the bite
- Red streaks spreading from the affected area

## GET PROFESSIONAL HELP IF

- An animal or human bite is on the face.
- A wound is large or appears infected.
- There is any chance the bite came from a rabies-infected animal. In such a case, try to have the animal captured and checked for rabies.
- A wound appears infected or extremely swollen.
- Breathing problems appear after an insect bite.
- Itching is severe or hives appear.

## WHAT TO CHECK

Keep an eye on your child following a bite and watch for signs of infection.

## TREATMENT

- Apply firm pressure, for up to five minutes, if you need to stop bleeding.
- Wash the bite area with soap and water.
- Use calamine lotion to soothe itching insect bites.
- For a bee or wasp sting, apply pressure with a cold, wet washcloth to reduce swelling. If you can see a stinger, try to remove it by scraping gently across the wound's surface.
- Trim your baby's fingernails to prevent scratching.

# Meningitis

## DESCRIPTION

A rare, but serious disease in which a bacteria or virus infects the membranes surrounding the brain and spinal cord.

## WHAT YOU NEED TO KNOW

Meningitis is a serious disease that should be diagnosed and treated by a physician as early as possible.

## SUPPLIES

Thermometer

## SYMPTOMS

- Moderate to high fever*
- Vomiting
- Decreased appetite
- Extreme listlessness or irritability
- Stiff neck (sometimes not in infants)
- Purple spots on body (sometimes)

## GET PROFESSIONAL HELP IF

- Meningitis symptoms are noted. No single symptom is indicative; look for the combination of symptoms listed.
- You are unsure or concerned; call your health care provider.

## WHAT TO CHECK

Do you know if your infant has been exposed to meningitis, in a day-care setting, for instance? Not all cases of meningitis are spread person-to-person, however.

## TREATMENT

Meningitis is a serious disease. It always requires a physician's care. See your health care provider immediately if you suspect meningitis.

- A spinal tap is necessary to confirm a diagnosis.
- Hospital admission and intravenous antibiotics, along with early identification, usually results in full recovery.

*See fever guide, pages 113–116.*

# Pinkeye (Conjunctivitis)

## DESCRIPTION

An irritation or infection of the conjunctiva, or eyelid lining.

## WHAT YOU NEED TO KNOW

- Many problems cause red eyes and discharge; pinkeye is only one of them.
- Infants with blocked tear ducts may be more susceptible to pinkeye.
- Ear infections can coexist with conjunctivitis.
- An infected eye will have discharge, in addition to being bloodshot and pinkish.
- Pinkeye can be very contagious.

## SUPPLIES

Prescribed antibiotics, cotton balls

## SYMPTOMS

- Red eyes
- Discharge from the eyes, often more abundant after sleep
- Swelling of eyelids

## GET PROFESSIONAL HELP IF

- Your infant has irritated or swollen eyes, and you are not sure of the cause. Typical causes include allergies, colds, chlorinated swimming pool water, dust, and blocked tear ducts.
- Your baby has recurrent eye irritations or discharge.

## WHAT TO CHECK

- Has your infant had contact with someone with pinkeye?
- Is increased tearing present from birth in one or both eyes?

## TREATMENT

- Home treatment should always be directed by your doctor. Different causes of pinkeye call for different therapies.
- Cotton balls wetted with clean water can be used to wipe away discharge.
- Wash your infant's hands frequently, and wash your hands after touching an infant with pinkeye.
- To protect other family members, isolate the baby's washcloth and towel.
- Discourage eye rubbing.

# Pneumonia

## DESCRIPTION

An infection of the lungs, usually viral but sometimes bacterial.

## WHAT YOU NEED TO KNOW

- Pneumonia has several different causes and can occur with greatly varying severity.
- Some forms of pneumonia are contagious; others are not.
- Common colds are rarely complicated by pneumonia.

## SUPPLIES

Thermometer, prescribed antibiotics (for some pneumonia), acetaminophen or ibuprofen

## SYMPTOMS

- Cough
- Fever* with sweating or chills
- Apparent stomach or chest pain
- Fast or labored breathing, indicated by flaring nostrils or wheezing
- Decreased appetite

## GET PROFESSIONAL HELP IF

You suspect pneumonia. Your doctor will diagnose the cause of the infection and may prescribe treatment. Very young children may need to be hospitalized.

## WHAT TO CHECK

Does your child seem to be working at breathing?

## TREATMENT

- If pneumonia is diagnosed, your doctor will treat it.
- Rest is important.
- Give expectorant cough medicines only if your doctor recommends them. In general, don't use a cough suppressant.
- Give acetaminophen or ibuprofen for fever. Contact your health care provider if fever is persistent.

*See fever guide, pages 113–116.*

# Poisoning

## DESCRIPTION

Swallowing of medicine, cleaning products, petroleum-based products, or other harmful substances can cause poisoning.

## WHAT YOU NEED TO KNOW

- Medicines, cleaners, house plants, and other common items are the chief causes of poisoning. (See pages 81–82.)
- Safe storage can prevent poisoning, but be ready for emergencies by posting your local poison-control center phone number in a handy location.

## SUPPLIES

Syrup of ipecac, water, milk

## SYMPTOMS

- Abdominal pain and diarrhea
- Blackouts and unconsciousness
- Convulsions or seizures
- Choking or difficulty breathing
- Confusion and drowsiness
- Coughing up blood and nausea
- Behavior change
- Rash or burns
- Excessive drooling
- Throat pain

## GET PROFESSIONAL HELP IF

You suspect your infant has swallowed or put any harmful substance in his mouth.

## WHAT TO CHECK

- Have any medicines, cleaners, or other harmful substances been opened, or are any missing? If you find a baby with an empty or open container of a dangerous substance, you should suspect poisoning.
- Take the container from which your baby took the substance and a sample of any vomit to the hospital with you. Make sure you keep it safely away from the infant.
- If you live in a dwelling with old paint in it, especially paint made before 1977, be sure to repaint it or frequently remove any chipping paint, as swallowing the paint chips could contribute to lead poisoning.

## TREATMENT

- Call the poison-control center immediately.
- Do not induce vomiting unless you are told to do so. Poison-control workers will give you instructions on how to use syrup of ipecac. (The usual dose is one tablespoon, followed by a glass of water.)

# Roseola

## DESCRIPTION

A fever and subsequent viral rash affecting young children and infants.

## WHAT YOU NEED TO KNOW

- Roseola is a common disease in infants six to twelve months of age.
- There is no prevention or cure, but it goes away on its own.
- The roseola rash follows about four days of high fever.
- Your infant will usually be well when the rash disappears, a day or two after it first appears.

## SUPPLIES

Thermometer, acetaminophen or ibuprofen, equipment for cool baths

## SYMPTOMS

- A high fever of 103 to 105°F (39.4 to 40.5°C)*
- Decreased appetite
- Mild crankiness or increased sleepiness
- Slightly raised, distinct red spots
- Rash generally appearing on trunk, upper arms, and neck

## GET PROFESSIONAL HELP IF

- Your child seems severely affected.
- Symptoms of roseola are accompanied by coughing, vomiting, or diarrhea.
- Low fever lasts longer than four days without other symptoms.

## WHAT TO CHECK

Any high fever requires close observation. Diagnosis of roseola can only be confirmed when rash appears. By then, if it is not roseola, complications could have occurred.

## TREATMENT

- Treat the fever with acetaminophen or ibuprofen and slightly cool baths.
- Watch your infant closely for other symptoms.
- Permit moderate activity if your child feels like it; it does no harm.

*See fever guide, pages 113–116.*

# Sudden Infant Death Syndrome (Crib Death)

## DESCRIPTION

The sudden death of an apparently normal, healthy infant during sleep for reasons that are unknown.

## WHAT YOU NEED TO KNOW

- SIDS usually occurs between four and sixteen weeks of life and its victims are more often boys than girls.
- SIDS is more common in premature infants, twins, those with a family history of SIDS, and those whose mothers smoke.
- The American Academy of Pediatrics recommends that babies sleep on their backs or sides rather than on their stomachs in hopes of decreasing the frequency of SIDS.

## SUPPLIES

A firm sleeping surface

## SYMPTOMS

None

## GET PROFESSIONAL HELP IF

- Your infant has bouts of sleep apnea—periods of twenty seconds or more when breathing stops.
- Your baby turns blue while sleeping.

## WHAT TO CHECK

- Is your baby's mattress too soft? Too-soft surfaces and fluffy bedding may be an increased risk factor.
- Is your baby's sleeping area too warm? Make sure the temperature is one you would feel comfortable sleeping in.

## TREATMENT

None. Parents of SIDS victims should seek local support through their health care provider.

# Teething

## DESCRIPTION

Tenderness of the gums of infants, caused by the eruption of teeth.

## WHAT YOU NEED TO KNOW

- Not all babies teethe at the same time; it depends on when their teeth erupt. (See pages 111–112.) Between three months and three years of age is typical.
- Never let a child go to sleep with a bottle of milk or juice. Doing so increases the risk of tooth decay.

## SUPPLIES

Thermometer, acetaminophen or ibuprofen, teething rings, teething biscuits, ice wrapped in a cloth

## SYMPTOMS

- Fussiness
- Drooling
- Chewing fingers or other objects
- Crying
- Low-grade fever, usually less than 100°F (37.8°C)*

## GET PROFESSIONAL HELP IF

Symptoms are accompanied by signs of illness, such as loss of appetite. Teething should not cause a high fever; if your baby has one, consider other causes. Otherwise, professional help is not needed for the eruption of teeth.

## WHAT TO CHECK

Consider other causes of symptoms: hunger, thirst, boredom, ear infection, a need for affection.

## TREATMENT

- Little can be done to help teething babies. Cuddling works as well as anything.
- You can try giving acetaminophen or ibuprofen to relieve gum soreness.
- Try offering some children teething rings or biscuits, which may help. Some teething babies like to chew cool objects (ice wrapped in cloth or a frozen teething ring). Avoid giving medications sold to relieve teething pain; their effectiveness is not proven.

*See fever guide, pages 113–116.*

153

# Thrush

## DESCRIPTION

A yeast infection of the mouth and tongue.

## WHAT YOU NEED TO KNOW

Thrush causes no symptoms except white patches on the mouth and tongue. It may go away if ignored, but most parents find they want to treat it.

## SUPPLIES

Prescribed medication

## SYMPTOMS

- White patches on the insides of the cheeks, behind the lips, or on the tongue
- Patches that look like dried milk, but will not wipe off with a clean handkerchief

## GET PROFESSIONAL HELP IF

Your infant has thrush or you suspect he does. This is not an urgent condition, however.

## WHAT TO CHECK

Are there blisters inside the infant's mouth? If so, it might be something other than thrush.

## TREATMENT

- Apply prescribed medication to patches as directed.
- Breastfeeding mothers may need to apply medicated ointment to their nipples in order to prevent reinfection.

# Urinary Tract Infection

## DESCRIPTION

An infection of the urinary system that can lead to a variety of problems or can be a symptom of other illnesses.

## WHAT YOU NEED TO KNOW

- Urinary tract infections can be tricky to detect and treat, especially in infancy.
- As newborns, both boys and girls can get these infections. Later on, girls are more at risk.
- A physician will often look for a urinary tract infection if there seems to be no other cause of persistent high fevers.

## SUPPLIES

Thermometer, acetaminophen or ibuprofen, juices

## SYMPTOMS

- Frequent, painful, or bloody urination
- Foul-smelling urine
- Apparent abdominal or back pain
- Fever*
- Nausea

## GET PROFESSIONAL HELP IF

- You detect any sign of urinary tract infection or blockage.
- Your infant has a fever over 101°F (38.3°C) or appears very ill.

## WHAT TO CHECK

If there is a family history of bladder or kidney problems, you should let your health care provider know.

## TREATMENT

- Until you see your doctor, give acetaminophen or ibuprofen for pain and administer large amounts of fluids.
- Your health care provider will test a urine sample to confirm the presence or absence of infection. If there is a urinary tract infection, further tests can determine any underlying causes.

*See fever guide, pages 113–116.

# Vomiting

## DESCRIPTION

The forceful expelling of food from the stomach through the nose and mouth—a common symptom with many causes.

## WHAT YOU NEED TO KNOW

- The most common cause of vomiting, by far, is a viral infection in the stomach.
- Infants often spit up—when contents flow easily out the mouth. Spitting up is not considered vomiting.
- The main concern with vomiting is dehydration.
- Vomiting in the first few months of life may have some specific underlying causes:
  —If it occurs thirty to forty-five minutes after every feeding, your baby may have pyloric stenosis, a condition where food cannot pass out of the stomach into the small intestine. This condition requires surgery.
  —Muscles at the entrance to the stomach may be especially relaxed, resulting in a condition known as reflux. A physician can discuss various treatments for this condition with you.

## SUPPLIES

Thermometers; commercial electrolyte mixes, such as Lytren, Pedialyte, Ricelyte, and Infalyte

## GET PROFESSIONAL HELP IF

- Any vomiting does not stop within twelve hours or is combined with drowsiness, apparent abdominal pain, high fever,* labored breathing.
- Vomited material is yellow or green more than once or twice.
- Your infant vomits forcefully shortly after being fed.

## WHAT TO CHECK

Look for signs of dehydration: listlessness, dry mouth, sunken eyes, crying without tears, infrequent urination.

## TREATMENT

- Watch infants under five months of age closely, and call your doctor if vomiting persists.
- Wait a while after your infant vomits. Then offer cool liquids in frequent, small amounts (one teaspoon to one tablespoon) at ten-minute intervals. The ideal solution is commercially available electrolyte preparations.
- Increase clear liquid intake gradually. Do not feed the child chicken broth, which contains fat and may be difficult to digest.
- Keep the child on clear liquids for a day. If your child is on solid food, allow light foods first (Jell-O, applesauce, dry toast, rice, bananas), then a regular diet.

*See fever guide, pages 113-116.

# Appendix

## Guide to Resources

### Books

Carter, John Mack (ed.), *The Good Housekeeping Illustrated Book of Pregnancy and Baby Care* (Hearst)

Einzig, Mitchell, *Baby and Child Emergency First-Aid Handbook* (Meadowbrook)

Eisenberg, Arlene and Sandee Hathaway, *What to Expect the First Year* (Workman)

Hart, Terril, *Baby and Child Medical Care* (Meadowbrook)

Johnson, Robert V. (ed.), *Mayo Clinic Complete Book of Pregnancy and Baby's First Year* (William Morrow & Co.)

Lansky, Vicki, *Feed Me! I'm Yours* (Meadowbrook)

Lansky, Vicki, *Practical Parenting Tips* (Meadowbrook)

Spock, Benjamin and Michael Rothenberg, *Spock's New Baby and Child Care* (Simon & Schuster)

### Magazines

*American Baby*
249 West 17th Street
New York, NY 10011
(212) 645-0067

Monthly, written for expectant and new mothers, emphasizing health, nutrition, fashion, beauty tips, and more.

*Baby Talk*
25 West 43rd Street
New York, NY 10036-7406
(212) 840-4200

Written for expectant and new mothers, focusing on the first year of life.

*Child*
110 Fifth Avenue
New York, NY 10011-5699
(212) 463-1000

Written for parents of children aged up to twelve, including articles on child development, behavior, health, nutrition, and education.

*Mothering*
P.O. Box 1690
Santa Fe, NM 87504
(505) 984-8116

Written for mothers, fathers, and health care workers, emphasizing self-care tips and ways of meeting and coping with the challenges of parenthood.

### Parenting
301 Howard Street, 17th Floor
San Francisco, CA 94105
(415) 546-7575

Written for the educated contemporary woman, emphasizing the demands of child rearing, personal growth, and family life.

### Parents'
685 Third Avenue
New York, NY 10017-4052
(212) 878-8700

Written for young women aged 18–34 with growing children.

### Working Mother
230 Park Avenue
New York, NY 10169-0005
(212) 551-9500

Written for contemporary working women with children under age eighteen.


## Resource Groups

### American Academy of Pediatrics (AAP)
141 Northwest Point Boulevard
P.O. Box 927
Elk Grove Village, IL 60009-0927
Phone: (708) 228-5005
Fax: (708) 228-5097
E-mail: kidsdocs@aap.org.
World-Wide Web: http://www.aap.org

Professional medical society of pediatricians and pediatric subspecialists. Subdivisions include Accident and Poison Prevention; Early Childhood, Adoption, and Dependent Care; and Infectious Diseases. Operates a small member library of books and journals on pediatric medicine, office practice, and child health care policy. Publishes newsletters, journals, reports, guides, and handbooks.

### American Red Cross National Headquarters (ARC)
431 18th Street Northwest
Washington, DC 20006
Phone: (202) 737-8300

Assists other Red Cross societies. Publishes booklets and an annual report.

**International Childbirth Education Association (ICEA)**
P.O. Box 20048
Minneapolis, MN 55420
Phone: (612) 854-8660
Toll-Free: (800) 624-4934 (for book orders only)
Fax: (612) 854-8772
World-Wide Web: http://www.metrixcom.com/icea/index/htm

Purpose is to further the educational, physical, and emotional preparation of expectant parents for childbearing and breastfeeding. Offers a teacher certification program for childbirth educators. Publishes literature pertaining to family-centered maternity care, including journals and pamphlets. Operates a mail order bookstore in Minneapolis, Minnesota, which makes available literature on all aspects of childbirth education and family-centered maternity care.

**La Leche League International (LLLI)**
1400 Meacham
Schaumburg, IL 60173
Phone: (708) 519-7730
Toll-Free: (800) LA-LECHE
Fax: (708) 519-0035
E-mail (to chat): lllol@library.ummed.edu
E-mail (to suscribe): listserv@library.ummed.edu
World-Wide Web: http://www.prarienet.org/llli/

Operates 550 breastfeeding resource centers in forty-eight countries. Promotes breastfeeding as an important element in the healthy development of the baby and mother, and as a means to encourage closer family relationships. Provides support through informal discussions and individualized counseling. Supplies information through publications, telephone service, and correspondence. Sponsors workshops, conferences, and seminars. Publishes booklets, journals, pamphlets, and books.

**National Committee for the Prevention of Child Abuse (NCPCA)**
332 South Michigan Avenue, Suite 1600
Chicago, IL 60604-4357
Phone: (312) 663-3520
Toll-Free: (800) CHILDREN
Fax: (312) 939-8962
E-mail: ncpca@childabuse.org

Seeks to stimulate greater public awareness of the influence, origins, nature, and effects of child abuse. Serves as a national advocate to prevent the neglect and physical, sexual, and emotional abuse of children. Conducts child abuse prevention programs. Publishes booklets, pamphlets, and journals.

### National Information Center for Children and Youth with Disabilities (NICHCY)

P.O. Box 1492

Washington, DC 20013

Phone: (202) 884-8200

Toll-Free: (800) 695-0285

Fax: (202) 884-8441

E-mail (to order publications list): gopher aed.org

E-mail (to ask questions): nichcy@aed.org

Provides information to assist parents, educators, advocates, and others in helping children and youth with disabilities participate as fully as possible in school, at home, and in the community. Offers personal responses to specific questions. Gives referrals to other organizations and sources of help. Offers technical assistance to parents and professional groups. Publishes booklets, a free newsletter, papers, and informational packets.

### National Institute of Mental Health (NIMH)

5600 Fishers Lane, Room 7-99

Rockville, MD 20857

Phone: (301) 443-3673

Fax: (301) 443-2578

Plans, conducts, fosters, and supports research, research training, and services on the brain, mental illness, and mental health, particularly the causes, prevention, diagnosis, and treatment of mental illness.

### Parents Anonymous

675 West Foothill Boulevard, Suite 220

Claremont, CA 91711-3416

Phone: (909) 621-6184

Fax: (909) 625-6304

E-mail: hn3831@handsnet.org

Works for the prevention and treatment of child abuse. Treatment blends support groups with self-help. Publishes a newsletter.

### Parents Without Partners, Inc. (PWP)

401 North Michigan Avenue

Chicago, IL 60611-4267

Phone: (312) 644-6610

Toll-Free: (800) 637-7974

Fax: (312) 321-6869

Researches single parent topics. Promotes the study and alleviation of the problems of single parents (custodial and noncustodial) in relation to the welfare and upbringing of their children and the acceptance into the general social order of single parents and their children. Publishes brochures and manuals.

**United States Consumer Product Safety Commission**
Washington, DC 20207
Toll-Free: (800) 638-2772
Fax: (301) 504-0051
E-mail (for general information): gopher services:cpse.gov
E-mail (to report products): info:cpse.gov

Provides information on the safety and effectiveness of consumer products.

**Consumer Product Safety Commission**
National Injury Information Clearinghouse
5401 Westbard Avenue
Bethesda, MD 20207
Phone: (301) 504-0424
Toll-Free: (800) 638-CPSC
Fax: (301) 504-0025

Clearinghouse that collects and disseminates injury data and information on the causes and prevention of death, injury, and illness associated with consumer products and maintains detailed investigative reports of such injuries.

**SIDS Alliance**
1314 Bedford Avenue, Suite 210
Baltimore, MD 21208
Phone: (410) 653-8226
Toll-Free: (800) 221-SIDS
Fax: (410) 653-8709

Serves as a central source of medical and scientific information about SIDS. Works to eliminate SIDS through research. Assists bereaved parents who have lost a child to SIDS. Works with families and professionals in caring for infants at risk due to cardiac and respiratory problems.

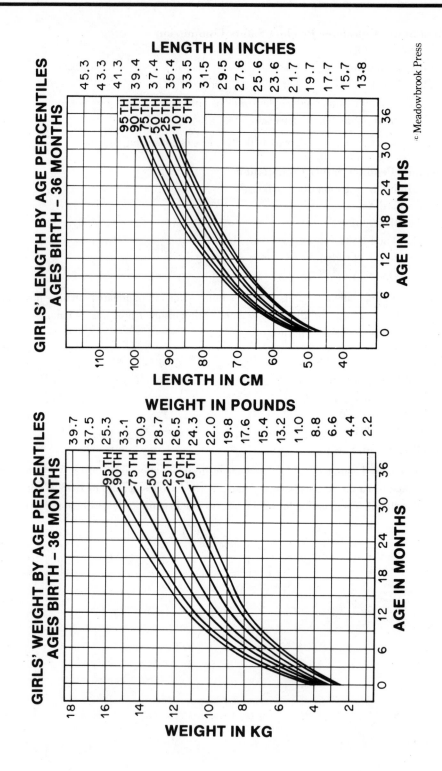

**LENGTH IN INCHES**

45.3 43.3 41.3 39.4 37.4 35.4 33.5 31.5 29.5 27.6 25.6 23.6 21.7 19.7 17.7 15.7 13.8

© Meadowbrook Press

**GIRLS' LENGTH BY AGE PERCENTILES
AGES BIRTH – 36 MONTHS**

95TH 90TH 75TH 50TH 25TH 10TH 5TH

**AGE IN MONTHS**

36  30  24  18  12  6  0

110  100  90  80  70  60  50  40

**LENGTH IN CM**

**WEIGHT IN POUNDS**

39.7 37.5 25.3 33.1 30.9 28.7 26.5 24.3 22.0 19.8 17.6 15.4 13.2 11.0 8.8 6.6 4.4 2.2

**GIRLS' WEIGHT BY AGE PERCENTILES
AGES BIRTH – 36 MONTHS**

95TH 90TH 75TH 50TH 25TH 10TH 5TH

**AGE IN MONTHS**

36  30  24  18  12  6  0

18  16  14  12  10  8  6  4  2

**WEIGHT IN KG**

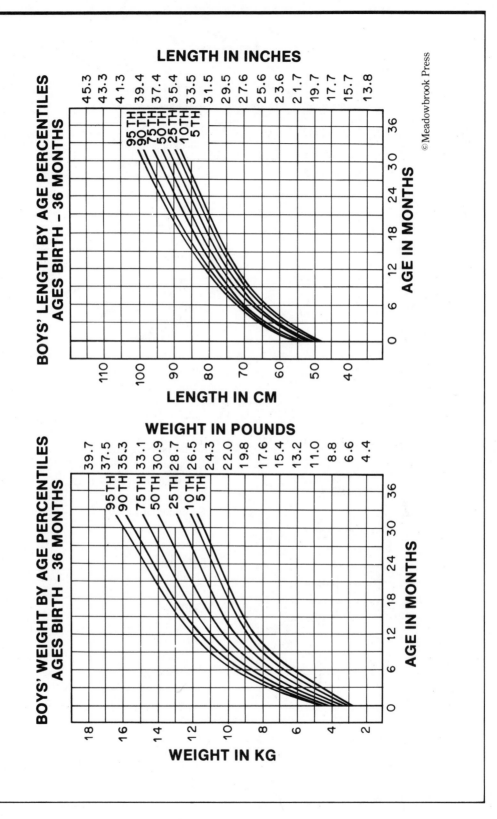

**LENGTH IN INCHES**

**BOYS' LENGTH BY AGE PERCENTILES AGES BIRTH – 36 MONTHS**

45.3 43.3 41.3 39.4 37.4 35.4 33.5 31.5 29.5 27.6 25.6 23.6 21.7 19.7 17.7 15.7 13.8

95 TH 90 TH 75 TH 50 TH 25 TH 10 TH 5 TH

110 100 90 80 70 60 50 40

**AGE IN MONTHS**

0 6 12 18 24 30 36

**LENGTH IN CM**

©Meadowbrook Press

**WEIGHT IN POUNDS**

**BOYS' WEIGHT BY AGE PERCENTILES AGES BIRTH – 36 MONTHS**

39.7 37.5 35.3 33.1 30.9 28.7 26.5 24.3 22.0 19.8 17.6 15.4 13.2 11.0 8.8 6.6 4.4

95 TH 90 TH 75 TH 50 TH 25 TH 10 TH 5 TH

18 16 14 12 10 8 6 4 2

**AGE IN MONTHS**

0 6 12 18 24 30 36

**WEIGHT IN KG**

# Index

See the symptoms index on page 117 for symptoms
associated with specific illnesses and injuries.

## A

Accident prevention
  *see safety*
Acetaminophen doses  . . . . . . . . 114–115
Acne, newborn . . . . . . . . . . . . . . . . . . 118
Activity box . . . . . . . . . . . . . . . . . . . . 106
Allergies, food . . . . . . . . . . . . . . . . . . 72
Apgar tests . . . . . . . . . . . . . . . . . . . . . 12

## B

Baby food, preparing . . . . . 63–64, 75–76
Babysitters . . . . . . . . . . . . . . . . . . . . . 88
Backpacks . . . . . . . . . . . . . . . . . . . . . . 85
Bathing
  sponge baths . . . . . . . . . . . . . . 30–31
  tub baths . . . . . . . . . . . . . . . . . 32–33
Bicycle seats . . . . . . . . . . . . . . . . . . . . 87
Birthmarks . . . . . . . . . . . . . . . . . . . . . 10
Bites . . . . . . . . . . . . . . . . . . . . . . . . . . 146
Biting . . . . . . . . . . . . . . . . . . . . . . . . . 55
  *see also teething*
Blocks, toy . . . . . . . . . . . . . . . . . . . . 105
Books
  board . . . . . . . . . . . . . . . . . . . . . . 105
  resource . . . . . . . . . . . . . . . . . . . . 159
Bottlefeeding . . . . . . . . . . . 2, 50, 61–70
Bowel movements . . . . . . . . . . . . . . . . 23
  *see also constipation, diarrhea*
Breastfeeding . . . . . . . . . . . . . . 2, 50–60
Breasts
  care of . . . . . . . . . . . . . . . . . . . . . . 54
  size of . . . . . . . . . . . . . . . . . . . . . . 51
Breathing emergency . . . . . . . . 119–120
Bronchiolitis . . . . . . . . . . . . . . . . . . 121
Burping . . . . . . . . . . . . . . . . . . . . 68–69

## C

Car seats . . . . . . . . . . . . . . . . . . . . . . 83
Cardiac arrest . . . . . . . . . . . . . 122–123
Carriages, baby . . . . . . . . . . . . . 84–85
Carriers, front . . . . . . . . . . . . . . . . . . 85
Changing table . . . . . . . . . . . . . . . . . 25

## Checkups
  medical . . . . . . . . . . . . . . . . . . . . 110
  schedule of . . . . . . . . . . . . . . . . . 110
  *see also immunizations, medical care*
Childproofing . . . . . . . . . . . . . . . 78–82
  *see also safety*
Choking . . . . . . . . . . . . . . . . . 124–125
Circumcision
  care . . . . . . . . . . . . . . . . . . . . . . . . 34
  making decision about . . . . . . . . . 2
Clothing
  buying . . . . . . . . . . . . . . . . . . . . . . 42
  checklist . . . . . . . . . . . . . . . . . 44–46
  newborn . . . . . . . . . . . . . . . . . 44–45
  older baby . . . . . . . . . . . . . . . 45–46
  shoes and socks . . . . . . . . . . . . . . 43
  waterproof pants . . . . . . . . . . . . . 25
Cold . . . . . . . . . . . . . . . . . . . . . . . . . 126
Colic . . . . . . . . . . . . . . . . 40, 127–128
Collar bone, broken . . . . . . . . . . . . . 10
Colostrum . . . . . . . . . . . . . . . . . . . . . 51
  *see also breastfeeding*
Concussion . . . . . . . . . . . . . . . . . . . . 129
Conjunctivitis
  *see pinkeye*
Constipation . . . . . . . . . . . . . . . . . . 130
Convulsions . . . . . . . . . . . . . . . . . . . 131
Cough . . . . . . . . . . . . . . . . . . . . . . . . 132
Cradle cap (seborrhea) . . . . . . . . . . 133
Cradle gym . . . . . . . . . . . . . . . . . . . 104
Cribs . . . . . . . . . . . . . . . . . . . . . . . . . 84
Crib death
  *see sudden infant death syndrome*
Crossed eyes . . . . . . . . . . . . . . . . . . 134
Croup . . . . . . . . . . . . . . . . . . . . . . . . 135
Crying, causes of and comforts for . . . . 40

## D

Daycare . . . . . . . . . . . . . . . . . . . . . . . 47
Dehydration . . . . . . . . . . . . . . . . . . . 136
Dental care . . . . . . . . . . . . . . . . 111–112
  *see also teeth, teething*

Development, baby .......... 91–108
    first month ............... 92–93
    second month ............ 92–93
    third month ............. 94–95
    fourth month ............ 94–95
    fifth month .............. 94–95
    sixth month ............. 96–97
    seventh month ........... 96–97
    eighth month ............. 96–98
    ninth month ............. 96, 98
    tenth month ............ 99–100
    eleventh month .......... 99–100
    twelfth month ........... 99–100
Diaper rash .................. 137
    *see also rashes*
Diapers .................... 25–29
    care of ..................... 27
    cloth .................... 25–27
    disposable .............. 25–27
    how to diaper ........... 28–29
Diarrhea .................. 138–139

**E**

Ear infection ................. 140
Eczema ..................... 141
    *see also rashes*
Engorgement ................ 54–55
    *see also breastfeeding*
Equipment, baby ............. 83–87
Exercises, baby ............ 107–108
Eyes
    blinking ................... 18
    newborn sight ......... 12, 14–15
    *see also crossed eyes, pinkeye*
Exams, newborn .............. 12–13
Expressing milk ................ 53

**F**

Feeding .................... 49–76
    *see also baby food, preparing; bottle-*
    *feeding; breastfeeding; food pyramid,*
    *solid foods*
Fever ..................... 113–115
    levels .................... 114
    treatment ................. 114
    *see also temperatures*
Fifth disease ................. 142
Fingernails, care of ............. 35
Food pyramid ................. 71
Football hold ............... 20, 59

Formula .................... 61–64
    *see also bottlefeeding*
Furniture
    *see equipment*

**G**

Gagging reflex .................. 18
Groups, resource ............ 160–163
Growth charts ............... 164–165

**H**

Handling babies
    holding .................... 20
    picking up ................. 21
    swaddling and rocking ........ 22
Head injury
    *see concussion*
Hearing
    newborn hearing ............. 15
    hearing loss ................ 143
Heat rash ..................... 144
    *see also rashes*
Heat stroke ................... 144
Hematoma .................... 10
Highchairs .................... 86
Hips, dislocated ................ 10
Home health care ................ 2

**I**

Immunizations ............. 110–111
Impetigo ..................... 145
Infant seats ................... 85
Intelligence .................... 15

**J**

Jaundice, newborn .............. 10
Jump-up harnesses .............. 87

**L**

Latching-on ................... 51
Length of newborns .............. 6
    *see also growth charts*
Let-down reflex ................ 52
Lip blisters ................... 10

**M**

Magazines, resource .......... 159–160
Massaging babies ............... 35
Mastitis ...................... 55
    *see also breastfeeding*

Medical care ............... 109–156
    *see also checkups, immunizations,*
    *home health care, symptoms index*
Meningitis .................... 147
Milia ......................... 10
Mobiles ...................... 102

## N

Navel care .................... 34
Newborn
    acne ..................... 118
    birth conditions ........... 10–11
    body characteristics ......... 8–9
    clothing ................. 44–45
    exams ................... 12–13
    length ...................... 6
    rash ....................... 11
    reflexes ................. 16–18
    screening tests ............. 13
    senses .................. 14–15
    weight ...................... 6
Nursery monitors ................. 86
Nursing
    *see breastfeeding*
Nursing mother's diet ............. 56
Nutrition
    *see feeding*

## P

Pacifiers ....................... 41
Penis care .................. 34–35
Pinkeye ...................... 148
Playpens ................. 86, 106
Pneumonia ................... 149
Poisoning .................... 150
    poisonous plants ........... 82
    poisonous substances ......... 81
Prickly heat .................. 144
    *see also rashes*

## R

Rashes
    diaper rash ............... 137
    eczema .................. 141
    fifth disease .............. 142
    heat rash (prickly heat) ....... 144
    newborn rash .............. 11
    roseola .................. 151
    *see also skin conditions*
Rattles ...................... 103

Reflexes, newborn ............. 16–18
Resources
    books ................... 159
    magazines ............. 159–160
    groups ............... 160–163
Rooting ....................... 16
    *see also breastfeeding*
Roseola ...................... 151
    *see also rashes*

## S

Safety ..................... 77–89
    bathroom ................. 80
    bedroom ................. 80
    kitchen/dining room .......... 79
    outside .................. 81
    poisoning ............... 150
    poisonous plants ........... 82
    poisonous substances ......... 81
    stairs .................. 80
    *see also childproofing*
Schedule, immunization .......... 111
Screening tests, newborn .......... 13
Seborrhea
    *see cradle cap*
Seizure ..................... 131
Shaking babies ................. 22
Shoes and socks ............... 43
    *see also clothing*
Shots
    *see immunizations*
Skin care .................. 34–35
Skin conditions
    cradle cap (seborrhea) ......... 133
    impetigo ................ 145
    newborn acne ............. 118
    *see also rashes*
Sleep ..................... 36–39
    positions during .......... 37–38
Smelling ..................... 15
Sociability ................... 15
Solid foods ................. 71–76
Spitting up ................. 68–69
Spoon-feeding ................. 74
Startle reflex ................. 16
Strollers .................. 84–85
Stuffed animals .............. 103
Sucking ................. 16, 40
    *see also breastfeeding, pacifiers, thumb*
    *sucking*

Sudden infant death syndrome  37–38, 152
Supplies, medical . . . . . . . . . . . . . . . . 113
Swaddling  . . . . . . . . . . . . . . . . . . . . . . 22
Swallowing . . . . . . . . . . . . . . . . . . . . . . 18
Symptoms index . . . . . . . . . . . . . . . . . 117

**T**

Tasting . . . . . . . . . . . . . . . . . . . . . . . . . 15
Tear ducts, blocked  . . . . . . . . . . . . . . 10
Teeth . . . . . . . . . . . . . . . . . . . . . . . . . 112
    *see also dental care and teething*
Teething . . . . . . . . . . . . . . . . . . . . . . . 153
Temperatures
    how to take  . . . . . . . . . . . . 115–116
    *see also fever*
Thrush . . . . . . . . . . . . . . . . . . . . . . . . 154
Thumb sucking  . . . . . . . . . . . . . . . . . 41
Toes, pigeon . . . . . . . . . . . . . . . . . . . . 11
Tongue tie  . . . . . . . . . . . . . . . . . . . . . 11
Tonic neck reflex . . . . . . . . . . . . . . . . 17
Toys . . . . . . . . . . . . . . . . . . . . 101–106
Traveling with babies . . . . . . . . . . . . . 89

**U**

Umbilical cord care
    *see navel care*
Urinary tract infection  . . . . . . . . . . . 155
Urination . . . . . . . . . . . . . . . . . . . . . . 23

**V**

Vitamin supplements . . . . . . . . . . . . . 75
Vomiting  . . . . . . . . . . . . . . . . . . . . . 156

**W**

Walkers . . . . . . . . . . . . . . . . . . . . . . . 87
Weaning
    from the breast  . . . . . . . . . . . . . 60
    from the bottle . . . . . . . . . . . . . . 70
Weight of newborns  . . . . . . . . . . . . . . 6
    *see also growth charts*
Wind-up swings . . . . . . . . . . . . . . . . . 87
Withdrawl reflex  . . . . . . . . . . . . . . . . 18
Wrist lesions  . . . . . . . . . . . . . . . . . . . 11

# Order Form

| Qty. | Title | Author | Order No. | Unit Cost (U.S. $) | Total |
|------|-------|--------|-----------|---------------------|-------|
| | 10,000 Baby Names | Lansky, B. | 1210 | $3.50 | |
| | Baby & Child Emergency First-Aid | Einzig, M. | 1380 | $8.00 | |
| | Baby & Child Medical Care | Hart, T. | 1159 | $8.00 | |
| | Baby Journal | Bennett, M. | 3172 | $10.00 | |
| | Baby Name Personality Survey | Lansky/Sinrod | 1270 | $8.00 | |
| | Best Baby Shower Book | Cooke, C. | 1239 | $7.00 | |
| | Childhood Medical Record Book | Fix, S. | 1130 | $10.00 | |
| | Discipline Without Shouting or Spanking | Wyckoff/Unell | 1079 | $6.00 | |
| | Familiarity Breeds Children | Lansky, B. | 4015 | $7.00 | |
| | Feed Me! I'm Yours | Lansky, V. | 1109 | $9.00 | |
| | First-Year Baby Care | Kelly, P. | 1119 | $9.00 | |
| | Gentle Discipline | Lighter, D. | 1085 | $6.00 | |
| | Getting Organized for Your New Baby | Bard, M. | 1229 | $9.00 | |
| | Grandma Knows Best | McBride, M. | 4009 | $5.00 | |
| | Hi, Mom! Hi, Dad! | Johnston, L. | 1139 | $6.00 | |
| | If We'd Wanted Quiet/Poems for Parents | Lansky, B. | 3505 | $12.00 | |
| | Joy of Parenthood | Blaustone, J. | 3500 | $6.00 | |
| | Practical Parenting Tips | Lansky, V. | 1180 | $8.00 | |
| | Pregnancy, Childbirth, and the Newborn | Simkin/Whalley/Keppler | 1169 | $12.00 | |
| | Very Best Baby Name Book | Lansky, B. | 1030 | $8.00 | |
| | Working Woman's Guide to Breastfeeding | Dana/Price | 1259 | $7.00 | |
| | | | | Subtotal | |
| | | | Shipping and Handling (see below) | | |
| | | | MN residents add 6.5% sales tax | | |
| | | | | **Total** | |

**YES!** Please send me the books indicated above. Add $2.00 shipping and handling for the first book and 50¢ for each additional book. Add $2.50 to total for books shipped to Canada. Overseas postage will be billed. Allow up to four weeks for delivery. Send check or money order payable to Meadowbrook Press. No cash or C.O.D.'s, please. Prices subject to change without notice. **Quantity discounts available upon request.**

Name _____

Address _____

City _____ State _____ Zip _____

Telephone (_____) _____

Purchase order number (if necessary) _____

**Payment via:**

☐ Check or money order payable to Meadowbrook Press (No cash or C.O.D.'s, please.) Amount enclosed $_____

☐ Visa (for orders over $10.00 only)     ☐ MasterCard (for orders over $10.00 only)

Account #_____

Signature _____ Exp. Date _____

A **FREE** Meadowbrook catalog is available upon request.
You can also phone us for orders of $10.00 or more at 1-800-338-2232.

**Mail to:**                    Meadowbrook, Inc.
18318 Minnetonka Boulevard, Deephaven, Minnesota 55391

Phone (612) 473-5400          Toll-Free 1-800-338-2232          Fax (612) 475-0736